A THEOLOGY OF THE
NEW TESTAMENT

A Theology of the New Testament

Timothy P. Palmer

AFRICA CHRISTIAN TEXTBOOKS

2012

A Theology of the New Testament

© 2012 Timothy P. Palmer

Africa Christian Textbooks (ACTS)

ACTS Bookshop, International HQ, TCNN,
PMB 2020, Bukuru, Plateau State, 930008, Nigeria
GSM: +234 (0) 803-589-5328; E-mail: pa@actsnigeria.org
Website: http://actsnigeria.org

ISBN: 9789789051489 Print
ISBN: 9789789053445 ePub
ISBN: 9789789053452 Mobi

CONTENTS

PREFACE

The New Testament is the primary witness to the life and teaching of Jesus of Nazareth. The New Testament contains the writings of some of the first witnesses of Jesus.

The New Testament is also the foundation of the Christian church. A knowledge of the New Testament is essential for those desiring to understand Christianity.

This book considers some of the main themes of the New Testament writings. This book follows the basic structure of George E. Ladd's *A Theology of the New Testament*. The reader is encouraged to consult Ladd or other evangelical sources for further reading.

This book is evangelical in its presuppositions. It is our assumption that the New Testament, together with the Old Testament, is the Word of God and therefore authoritative for life and for doctrine.

This book is a result of my teaching at the Theological College of Northern Nigeria. I am deeply thankful to the proprietors of TCNN who have allowed me to teach at this fine institution for more than 25 years. I am also thankful to the students of TCNN who have interacted in a lively way in the classroom. It has been a great privilege to study the Scriptures with such committed students.

It is my prayer that this book will be useful for a deeper understanding of the New Testament.

Christmas 2011
Theological College of Northern Nigeria
Bukuru

PART I

THE SYNOPTIC GOSPELS

The Synoptic Gospels, together with John's Gospel, are our primary source for the life of Jesus. The three Synoptic Gospels are Mark, Matthew and Luke. The word "synoptic" is a Greek expression meaning to "see together." (*Syn* means "together"; *optic* refers to "seeing.") The three Synoptic Gospels give similar but different views of the life of Jesus.

As evangelicals, we believe that each Gospel is inspired by God. Thus the three Gospels complement each other but do not contradict each other. Each gives a slightly different perspective of who Jesus is.

The Synoptic Gospels were probably written between 60 and 80 A.D. It is generally assumed that Mark's Gospel, which is the shortest, was written first. Mark's Gospel gives the basic historical facts of Jesus' life. Matthew and Luke add a number of sayings and parables of Jesus. The sayings that are common to Matthew and Luke are sometimes called "Q", from the German word for "source," *Quelle.*

CHAPTER 1

JOHN THE BAPTIZER

Mark's account of Jesus begins with John the baptizer. The gospels of Matthew and Luke also start with John, after the birth narratives. So who was John? Why was he important?

John was a unique person. He was dressed with camel's hair and a leather belt and he ate locusts and wild honey (Mk 1:6). This reminds us of the prophet Elijah who also wore a garment of hair and a leather belt (2 Kgs 1:8). This suggests that John was a prophet like the Old Testament prophets.

The end of an age

When John was in prison Jesus spoke of him, "Among those born of women there has not risen anyone greater than John the Baptist; yet the one who is least in the kingdom of heaven is greater than he" (Mt 11:11/Lk 7:28).[1] This is puzzling. Are we today greater than John the baptizer?

Jesus then suggests that there are two distinct ages or eras in salvation history. "From the days of John the Baptist until now,

---

[1] All Scripture quotations are based on the New International Version, sometimes modified to reflect better the sense of the original Greek. The abbreviation "par." refers to parallel texts in other Gospels.

the kingdom of heaven has been forcefully advancing . . . . For all the prophets and the law prophesied until John" (Mt 11:12-13). Or, according to Luke, "The law and the prophets were proclaimed until John. Since that time the good news of the kingdom of God is being preached" (Lk 16:16).

The old age is that of the Old Testament law and prophets. The new era is that of the kingdom of God. But where does John the baptizer fit?

Jesus says that the smallest person in the kingdom of heaven is greater than John. Thus if your child sings "Jesus loves me" from the heart, she or he is greater than John the baptizer. John was the last great prophet of the old age.

The Baptism of John

So what was John's role? Why was he baptizing? We find an answer in the first words of John and of Jesus. In Matthew, both John and Jesus proclaim, "Repent, for the kingdom of heaven is near" (Mt 3:2; 4:17). The first words of Jesus in Mark's Gospel are, "The time has come. The kingdom of God is near. Repent and believe the good news" (Mk 1:15).

John was the last great prophet of the old covenant. A new era was at hand. The kingdom of God was near! Jesus was bringing this kingdom to the earth!

Matthew and Luke use eschatological language to describe the coming of Jesus. John proclaims that "the ax is already at the root of the trees, and every tree that does not produce good fruit will be cut down and thrown into the fire" (Mt 3:10/Lk 3:9). These words point to the final eschatological judgment.

Then John says that he baptizes with water but Jesus will baptize with the Holy Spirit and fire (Mt 3:11/ Lk 3:16).

The baptism of the Spirit is the outpouring of the Spirit prophesied by the Old Testament prophets. But what is the baptism by fire in this text?

Some assume that this is the fire of Pentecost. But probably it is the eschatological fire of judgment. The next verse explains the fire. "His winnowing fork is in his hand, and he will clear his threshing floor, gathering the wheat into his barn and burning up the chaff with unquenchable fire" (Mt 3:12/Lk 3:17). The unquenchable fire is the fire of the last judgment.

At the end, "a separation is to take place: some will be gathered into the divine granary—theirs will be a baptism of the Spirit; others will be swept away in judgment—theirs will be a baptism of fire.[2]

John was prophesying the end of time. He believed that the Messiah would usher in the final kingdom of God. The Messiah would bring the final redemption and judgment. John's message was thus eschatological, prophesying the end of time.

So if the end of time was near, repentance was urgent. If one did not repent, he or she would face the fires of judgment. So it is imperative that one repent from one's sinful life.

So what was the significance of John's baptism? John's baptism was a ceremonial washing to prepare for the coming kingdom. "John's baptism was eschatological in character, i.e., its *raison d'être* was to prepare people for the coming Kingdom. It is this fact which gives to John's baptism its unrepeatable character."[3]

John's baptism was not a proselyte baptism, because it was administered to Jews as well as Gentiles. John's baptism was not a Christian baptism, because it was not a baptism in the name of the Father, Son and Holy Spirit. Christian baptism began at Pentecost.

---

[2]G.E. Ladd, *A Theology of the New Testament*, p. 34.
[3]G.E. Ladd, *A Theology of the New Testament*, p. 38.

Instead, John's baptism was a messianic, eschatological baptism. It was preparation for the coming eschatological kingdom.

The Baptism of Jesus

So why was Jesus baptized? Jesus was baptized as a sign that the kingdom was near. Something brand new was going to happen. The kingdom of God was at hand. One writer speaks of "the eschatological significance of the baptism of Jesus."[4]

But the baptism of Jesus was also significant since the Spirit of God descended on him. "In the Judaism of the time, the imparting of the Spirit almost always means prophetic inspiration." So, when the Spirit descended on Jesus, "the meaning is that Jesus is called in this way to be God's messenger."[5]

During the baptism of Jesus there was a divine proclamation: "You are my beloved Son; in you I am well pleased" (Mk 1:11, par.). In this event "God was taking [Jesus] into his service, equipping him and authorizing him to be his messenger and the inaugurator of the time of salvation. At his baptism, Jesus experienced his call."[6]

Something new was going to happen. The Messiah was present, anointed by the Holy Spirit. The kingdom of God was near. It was time to repent.

---

[4]J. Jeremias, *New Testament Theology*, p. 53.
[5]J. Jeremias, *New Testament Theology*, p. 52.
[6]J. Jeremias, *New Testament Theology*, p. 55.

Study Questions

1. What does John's unique behavior tell us about him?
2. How are you greater than John the Baptist?
3. How is John's baptism eschatological in nature?
4. How will Jesus baptize with fire?
5. Why was Jesus baptized?

CHAPTER 2

THIS EVIL AGE

The world that Jesus met in his incarnation and ministry was an evil world. The world was full of demons with Satan as their leader. There was evil in the human world both at the individual and at the social level.

The Demons

In the Old Testament there are only about three places that speak of evil spirits.[1] But the Synoptic Gospels are full of references to these spirits. The brief gospel of Mark has more references to evil spirits than the entire Old Testament.

An evil spirit is often called a demon (*daimōn* or *daimonion*); sometimes it is called an evil or unclean spirit. Demons are "evil supernatural spirits."[2]

Demons often possessed a person and caused physical and spiritual torment. A significant part of the ministry of Jesus and his disciples was the casting out of demons.

Many Europeans today deny the existence of these spirits. One German theologian claimed that "now that the forces and the laws

---

[1] See T. Palmer, *A Theology of the Old Testament*, pp. 51-52.
[2] G.E. Ladd, *A Theology of the New Testament*, p. 49.

of nature have been discovered, we can no longer believe in spirits, whether good or evil."[3]

But Osadolor Imasogie calls this a quasi-scientific worldview since it excludes much of the spiritual world. He believes that we should teach and preach that "Christ is not only the all-sufficient saviour from the power of sin but also the all-sufficient conqueror of demons and deliverer from all fears."[4]

Satan

The leader of the demons is Satan. He is called "the prince of demons" (Mk 3:22). Satan rules over a kingdom which opposes God (cf. Mk 3:24-26).

The name Satan (*satanas*) comes from a Hebrew word which means accuser.[5] The other title for Satan is the devil (*diabolos*).

"The chief function of Satan in the Gospels is to oppose the redemptive purpose of God."[6] At the beginning of his ministry Jesus was tempted by Satan (Mk 1:12-13). Right after his magnificent confession, Peter was tempted by Satan (Mk 8:33). During Jesus' last week on earth, Satan tempted Judas and again Peter (Lk 22:3,31).

Satan or the Devil is the one who sows weeds in the field (Mt 13:39). He is also the one who snatches the seed or the word that is sown (Mk 4:15).

---

[3]R. Bultmann, "New Testament and Mythology," in *Kerygma and Myth*, p. 4. He adds: "It is impossible to use electric light and the wireless and to avail ourselves of modern medical and surgical discoveries, and at the same time to believe in the New Testament world of spirits and miracles" (p. 5).
[4]O. Imasogie, *Guidelines for Christian Theology in Africa*, p. 80.
[5]See T. Palmer, *A Theology of the Old Testament*, pp. 50-51.
[6]G.E. Ladd, *A Theology of the New Testament*, p. 47.

Satan was the one who kept a woman crippled for eighteen years (Lk 13:16). As the prince of demons he is responsible for much of the misery in our world.

There is thus an ethical dualism in the Synoptic Gospels between the kingdom of God and the kingdom of Satan. (An ethical dualism is a contrast between good and evil.) There is also warfare between the two kingdoms. Jesus said, "If I drive out demons by the finger of God, then the kingdom of God has come to you" (Lk 11:20).

When Jesus entered the synagogue in Capernaum, an evil spirit was afraid of Jesus. The spirit asked Jesus, "Have you come to destroy us?" (Mk 1:24). An essential part of the ministry of Jesus and the disciples was the casting out of demons. When the 72 disciples reported that the demons submitted to them, Jesus said, "I saw Satan fall like lightning from heaven" (Lk 10:18).

Satan and his kingdom have power; but Jesus' power and kingdom are greater. The advance of the kingdom of God means the defeat of the kingdom of Satan.

The Evil Heart

Of course not all evil is outside of us. The heart is the source of good and evil. Jesus said,

> From within, out of a person's heart, come evil thoughts, sexual immorality, theft, murder, adultery, greed, malice, lewdness, envy, slander, arrogance and folly
>
> —Mk 7:21-22

Satan is the evil one (Mt 6:13), but there are also evil persons (Mt 5:39). Even the religious leaders in Jesus' day were once called evil (Mt. 12:34).

Jesus compared people to good and evil trees.

> Every good tree bears good fruit, but a bad tree bears bad
> fruit. . . . Every tree that does not bear good fruit is cut down
> and thrown into the fire.
>
> —Mt 7:17,19

The society in Jesus' day had many sinners. The corrupt tax collectors and the prostitutes were prominent examples. But it was these people who often repented and found salvation. Zacchaeus (Lk 19:9) and a sinful woman (Lk 7:47-50) are examples of sinners who repented.

The Pharisees, on the other hand, were confident of their own righteousness. But typically it was the corrupt tax collector who repented and went home justified instead of the Pharisee (Lk 18:14).

The Synoptic Gospels speak of sins that need forgiveness. John's baptism was a preparation for the forgiveness of sins (Mk 1:4-5). John came to give people "the knowledge of salvation through the forgiveness of their sins" (Lk 1:77). Jesus forgave the sins of the paralytic man (Mk 2:5) and the sinful woman (Lk 7:48). The Lord's Prayer also contains the request, "Forgive us our sins" (Lk 11:4).

The world was indeed a sinful and evil world. There was a need for a Messiah to redeem mankind from their sins.

Study Questions

1. Describe the kingdom of Satan.
2. Why is the European worldview which denies spirits quasi-scientific?
3. What constitutes an evil person in the Gospels?
4. In the story of the Pharisee and the tax-collector (Lk 18:9-14), explain who the real sinner is.
5. In the parable of the prodigal son (Lk 15:11-32), explain which son is the sinner.

CHAPTER 3

THE KINGDOM OF GOD

The heart of Jesus' teaching is the kingdom or reign of God. His ministry began with the dramatic words, "The time has come. The reign (or kingdom) of God is near" (Mk 1:15). What is this kingdom that Jesus proclaimed?

The Jewish Expectation

The Old Testament looked forward to the coming kingdom of God. There were many prophecies of a future time of salvation.[1] These prophecies were eschatological, expecting the future or end times.

Many of these prophecies included the expectation of the Messiah. The Messiah would be the future king who would bring in the reign of God.

The prophet Amos expected a time in the future when David's fallen tent would be restored. It would be a time of agricultural abundance (Amos 9:11-15).

The prophet Isaiah looked forward to a time in the last days when the mountain of Yahweh's temple would be established. God's law would go out from Zion and there would be peace (Is 2:2-4).

---

[1]See T. Palmer, *A Theology of the Old Testament*, pp. 125-31.

The prophet Isaiah also expected a time when a descendant of David would rule in justice and righteousness. The result would be peace (Is 11:1-9).

The prophet Jeremiah anticipated the reign of a Davidic king who would rule with justice and righteousness (Jer 23:5-6).

The prophet Ezekiel prophesied a future time when God's Spirit would give the people a new heart and a new spirit. It would also be a time of agricultural plenty (Ezek 36:24-30). The king at that time would be a son of David (Ezek 37:24-28).

The prophet Joel expected the outpouring of the Spirit of God before the climatic day of Yahweh (Joel 2:28-32).

The prophet Zechariah prophesied a future day of Yahweh when God would reign. During his reign the nations would be defeated and Jerusalem would be secure (Zech 14).

These prophecies are eschatological. They looked forward to the future coming of God. In the future God would come to save. God would come to deliver his people. God would set up a kingdom for his saints. The Messiah would be there to bring salvation. The Messiah would establish the kingdom of God.

In the intertestamental period the Jews developed these expectations. Apocalyptic Judaism in particular expected God to intervene in history in the future in a dramatic way and to save his people.[2]

> Throughout all Judaism, the coming of God's kingdom was expected to be an act of God . . . to defeat the wicked enemies of Israel and to gather Israel together, victorious over its enemies, in its promised land, under the rule of God alone.
>
> —G.E. Ladd, *A Theology of the New Testament*, p. 60

---

[2]See G.E. Ladd, *A Theology of the New Testament*, pp. 58-60.

The presupposition of these expectations is a two-age structure. The old age is evil; but the new age would be a future time of salvation. This diagram represents the two-age structure of the Old Testament and the Jews.[3]

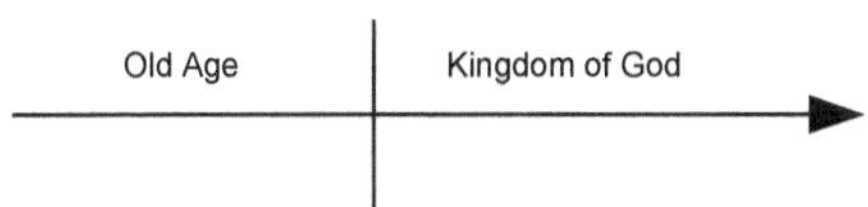

The Presence of God's Kingdom

So when Jesus began his ministry by saying that the kingdom of God is near, this was an amazing claim. Was God's glorious kingdom going to be established at that time?

John the baptizer, for example, was confused. While he was in prison, he heard reports about Jesus' ministry. But this Jesus was not the glorious king that John expected. So was Jesus indeed the Messiah?

Jesus sent a message to John saying that he was fulfilling the prophecy of Isaiah 35. The blind are seeing, the lame are walking, the lepers are being cured and the dead are being raised (Mt 11:5/Lk 7:22). Jesus continued by saying that the kingdom of heaven is now

---

[3]See G.E. Ladd, *A Theology of the New Testament*, p. 66.

forcefully advancing (Mt 11:12). The eschatological kingdom of God is now present! But it was present in a different way than the Jewish people expected.

Jesus began his ministry by "preaching the good news of the kingdom, and healing every disease and sickness among the people" (Mt 4:23). The kingdom of God was present, and the evidence of this kingdom was the healing of the sick.

Some time later, Jesus sent out the twelve apostles with the same message: "Preach this message, 'The kingdom of heaven is near.' Heal the sick, raise the dead, cleanse the lepers, drive out demons" (Mt 10:7-8).

On a different occasion, Jesus sent out 72 disciples with the same message. On their return they reported with astonishment that even the demons submitted to them. Jesus told them that he saw Satan fall like lightning from heaven (Lk 10:18).

The defeat of Satan and his demons is an indication that the kingdom of God is already present. Jesus said, "If I drive out demons by the Spirit of God, then the kingdom of God has come upon you" (Mt 12:28). In Luke we read, "If I drive out demons by the finger of God, then the kingdom of God has come to you" (Lk 11:20).

The eschatological kingdom of God began when Jesus started his ministry on earth. But this kingdom began in a quiet way. It is like a mustard seed which a man planted which took years to grow (Mt 13:31-32). It is like yeast in a batch of dough which took time to rise (Mt 13:33). It is like seed sown in a field which took a whole season to grow (Mt 13:24-30).

Jesus spoke of the presence of the kingdom once in a dialogue with the Pharisees. When they asked when the kingdom of God would come, Jesus said that "the kingdom of God is among you (*entos humōn*)" (Lk 17:20-21).

The amazing teaching of Jesus was that the eschatological kingdom of God had already come with the first coming of Jesus.

The Future Kingdom of God

Although God's kingdom is already present, its consummation is still in the future. Jesus still looked forward to the perfect kingdom of God in the future.

Jesus said that in the future "many will come from the east and the west and will take their places at the feast with Abraham, Isaac and Jacob in the kingdom of heaven" (Mt 8:11).

In the future some will "see Abraham, Isaac and Jacob and all the prophets in the kingdom of God" and many "will take their places at the feast in the kingdom of God" (Lk 13:28-29).

In the future the disciples will "eat and drink at Jesus' table in his kingdom, judging the twelve tribes of Israel" (Lk 22:29-30). In the future Jesus would drink of the fruit of the vine in the kingdom of God (Mk 14:25).

In the future the blessed ones will inherit the kingdom prepared for them from the foundation of the world (Mt 25:34). In the future those who are faithful will "inherit eternal life" or "enter the kingdom of God" (Mk 10:17,23).

There is then a mystery (*mustērion*) in the kingdom of God. Jesus spoke of "the mystery" or "mysteries" of the kingdom of God (Mk 4:11, par.). What is this mystery?

The mystery is the fact that the kingdom of God is already but not yet present. The mystery is that the kingdom is already present before its future culmination. "The mystery of the kingdom is the coming of the kingdom into history in advance of its apocalyptic manifestation. It is . . . 'fulfillment without consummation.'"[4]

---

[4] G.E. Ladd, *A Theology of the New Testament*, p. 91

In the Synoptic Gospels there is a modified two-age structure. A believer lives both in the old age and the new age at the same time. A believer is part of the old age, awaiting the kingdom of God; but the believer is also part of the new age of God's kingdom.

There is thus an "already"-"not yet" dynamic in Jesus' teaching about the kingdom of God. The kingdom of God is already but not yet present. The following diagram illustrates our present situation:[5]

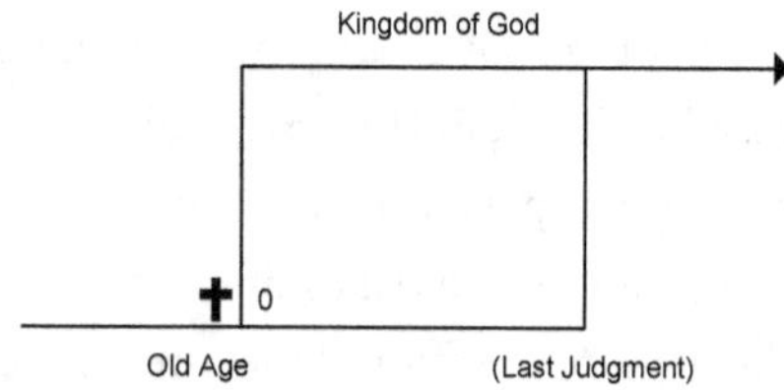

A Kingdom of Grace

So what is this new kingdom like?

"The kingdom of heaven is like a king who wanted to settle accounts with his servants" (Mt 18:23). But one of the servants who received forgiveness refused to forgive. The kingdom of God is a realm of forgiveness.

---

[5]See G. Vos, *The Pauline Eschatology*, p. 38; G.E. Ladd, *A Theology of the New Testament*, pp. 66-67. The symbols represent the cross and the empty tomb.

"The kingdom of heaven is like a landowner who went out early in the morning to hire men to work in his vineyard" (Mt. 20:1). The workers discovered the surprising quality of grace from the master.

"The kingdom of heaven is like a king who prepared a wedding banquet for his son" (Mt 22:2). Anyone was welcome, but they had to be properly dressed.

"The kingdom of heaven is like ten virgins who took their lamps and went out to meet the bridegroom" (Mt 25:1). But five were prepared and five were not.

The kingdom is like a man who went on a journey and entrusted talents to his servants (Mt 25:14). But some were faithful and others not.

The reign of God among us is a reign of forgiveness and grace. But it depends upon a faithful and gracious response to God's grace.

The Greek word for kingdom is basileia, which means both "rule" and "realm." The kingdom of God is God's rule or presence in Jesus; but it is also the realm of those who believe in Jesus.

The kingdom of God is a realm into which believers enter. "Unless you change and become like little children, you will never enter the kingdom of heaven" (Mt 18:3).

The kingdom is also a gift that a believer will inherit. We are to "receive the kingdom of God like a little child" (Mk 10:15). The kingdom is our "inheritance" prepared for us since the creation of the world (Mt 26:34).

In conclusion, the kingdom of God is God's reign both now and in the future. The kingdom of God is the realm of salvation and grace that we experience now and in the future.

Study Questions

1. Describe the eschatological hope of the Old Testament people.
2. What is evidence of the present kingdom of God among us?
3. What is the mystery of the kingdom?
4. Who will enter the kingdom of God?
5. What does the parable of the tares (or weeds) in Matthew 13:24-30 tell us about the kingdom of God?
6. What does the parable of the unmerciful servant in Matthew 18:21-35 tell us about the kingdom of God?
7. What does the parable of the ten virgins in Matthew 25:1-13 tell us about the kingdom of God?

CHAPTER 4

JESUS THE MESSIAH

Once when he was at Caesarea Philippi, Jesus asked the disciples, "Who do people say I am?" Then he asked them, "Who do you say I am?" (Mk 8:27-29).

This is one of the basic questions in New Testament theology —who indeed is Jesus of Nazareth? Who is Jesus according to the Synoptic Gospels?

Messiah

The personal name of our Savior is Jesus. It is derived from the Hebrew word for "save" or "savior." Thus, when he was born, the angel told his mother to call him Jesus "because he will save his people from their sins" (Mt 1:21).

But this Jesus was called "the Christ." Christ or *Christos* was initially a title, not a name. *Christos* is a Greek translation of the Hebrew word for Messiah. Usually, before his resurrection, *Christos* is used as a title: "the Messiah." But after his resurrection, *Christos* became a second personal name for Jesus: "Jesus Christ."

Jesus did not call himself the Messiah. This was because the Jewish people were expecting a royal messiah who would bring political deliverance to Israel. Jesus was not a political messiah.

But on two significant occasions in the Synoptic Gospels, Jesus agreed that he was the Messiah.[1] When Jesus asked the disciples who people thought he was, Peter responded boldly, "You are the Messiah (*Christos*)" (Mk 8:29). (Note the use of *Christos* as a title.)

Jesus agreed that he was the Messiah, but he told his disciples not to tell anyone (Mk 8:30). This is the messianic secret. Jesus wanted to keep his messianic identity secret so that he would not be crowned as a political king.

At the end of his life, Jesus was on trial before the Sanhedrin. The high priest then asked him, "Are you the Messiah, the Son of the Blessed One?" (Mk 14:61). Jesus then agreed that he was the Messiah. He said, "I am, and you will see the Son of Man sitting at the right hand of the Mighty One and coming on the clouds of heaven" (Mk 14:62).

There was then no more danger that Jesus would be crowned as a king. Instead, he was on the path to his death. So Jesus was then free to reveal his messianic identity.

Jesus knew that he was the Messiah but he was reluctant to say so directly. So what was Jesus' preferred title for himself?

Son of Man

Jesus' preferred title for himself is Son of Man. We find this term about 65 times in the Gospels. This term is Jesus' favorite way of designating himself. The title is never used by anyone else of Jesus in the Gospels. (Only Stephen used it at his martyrdom [Acts 7:56].)

So what does Son of Man mean? In the Old Testament, the prophet Ezekiel was called son of man about 93 times. This was God's particular way of addressing Ezekiel as a human prophet.

---

[1] Also in John's Gospel Jesus told the Samaritan woman that he was the Messiah (Jn 4:25-26).

But the decisive Old Testament passage for the Synoptic Gospels is Daniel 7. Here Daniel had a vision of God seated on the throne. Then he saw

> One like a son of man, coming with the clouds of heaven. He approached the Ancient of Days and . . . was given authority, glory and sovereign power.
>
> —Dan 7:13-14

This is a picture of the glorious, apocalyptic Son of Man. The Son of Man here is "a heavenly messianic eschatological figure who brings the kingdom to the afflicted saints on earth."[2]

When Jesus called himself the Son of Man, he was undoubtedly thinking of the Daniel passage. The term suggests his messianic identity.

But a study of the usage of Son of Man in the Synoptic Gospels reveals a new understanding of this concept. There are three categories of Son of Man sayings in the Synoptic Gospels.[3]

The first category is the earthly Son of Man. Jesus said, "Foxes have holes and birds of the air have nests, but the Son of Man has no place to lay his head" (Mt 8:20/Lk 9:58). This is an unusual Messiah. He appears different than the glorious Son of Man of Daniel.

This Son of Man came for a purpose. In one parable, it is the Son of Man who sows the seed (Mt 13:37). Luke tells us that "the Son of Man came to seek and to save what was lost" (Lk 19:10). The Son of Man even has authority to forgive sins (Mk 2:10).

Jesus redefined the Jewish idea of the messianic Son of Man. This Son of Man has a mission to perform on earth before entering into the state of glory.

---

[2]G.E. Ladd, *A Theology of the New Testament*, p. 147.
[3]See G.E. Ladd, *A Theology of the New Testament*, pp. 147-55.

This is clear in the second category of sayings. Jesus is not only the earthly Son of Man but also the suffering Son of Man. This is a radical redefinition of the concept of the Son of Man.

After Peter's great confession of Jesus as the Messiah, Jesus then said "that the Son of Man must suffer many things and be rejected . . . and that he must be killed" (Mk 8:31). For Peter this was incomprehensible. So Peter rebuked Jesus! But Jesus in turn rebuked Peter. The Son of Man would be a suffering Messiah.

The second and third predictions of the suffering and death of the Son of Man repeat this idea (Mk 9:31; Mk 10:33). The passion story reaffirms that the Son of Man would be betrayed (Mk 14:21,41).

The suffering of the Son of Man had a redemptive purpose: "The Son of Man did not come to be served but to serve and give his life as a ransom for many" (Mk 10:45).

Only after his suffering would Jesus be the glorious Son of Man. (This is the third category of sayings.) After telling Peter and the disciples that the Son of Man must suffer, Jesus spoke of the time when the Son of Man would come in his Father's glory with the holy angels (Mk 8:38).

In the passages on the signs of the end of the age, Jesus predicted the darkening of the sun and the moon. "At that time people will see the Son of Man coming in clouds with great power and glory" (Mk 13:26). This is the glorious, apocalyptic Son of Man that the Jews expected.

Matthew and Luke tell more about the glorious Son of Man. His coming will be like the lightning flashing from east to west. He will appear in the sky, and all the nations will mourn. He will come unexpectedly and gloriously (Mt 24:27-44/Lk 17:22-30).

When the high priest asked Jesus if he was the Messiah, Jesus said that in the future he would see the Son of Man "sitting at the right hand of the Mighty One and coming on the clouds of heaven" (Mk 14:62).

Jesus was the messianic Son of Man. But he redefined this traditional concept by bringing in the suffering servant idea of Isaiah 53. He was the earthly and suffering Son of Man before he was the glorious Son of Man.

Son of God

The Gospel of Mark was written with the belief that Jesus was also the Son of God. The Gospel opens: "The beginning of the Gospel about Jesus Christ, the Son of God" (Mk 1:1). Towards the end of this same Gospel, the centurion confesses, "Surely this man was the Son of God" (Mk 15:39).

In a few key passages in the Synoptic Gospels, Jesus is called the Son of God. At the baptism of Jesus, a voice from heaven said, "You are my beloved Son; in you I am well pleased" (Mk 1:11). At Jesus' transfiguration, a voice from heaven again said, "This is my beloved Son" (Mk 9:7).

At the beginning of his ministry, it was Satan and the evil spirits who already knew Jesus' identity as the Son of God. An evil spirit at Capernaum shouted, "I know who you are, the Holy One of God" (Mk 1:24). The evil spirits also cried out, "You are the Son of God" (Mk 3:11).

At Jesus' temptation, Satan said, "If you are the Son of God, tell these stones to become bread" (Mt 4:3/Lk 4:3). He also said, "If you are the Son of God, throw yourself down" (Mt 4:6/Lk 4:9).

At Jesus' trial, he was asked whether he was the Messiah, "the Son of the Blessed One" (Mk 14:61). At this point Jesus agreed that he was not only Messiah and glorious Son of Man but also the Son of God.

The Synoptic Gospels contain a vital testimony to the identity of Jesus. Jesus knew that he was the Messiah and the Son of God. But generally to avoid the political expectations of the Jews he used the more ambiguous "Son of Man."

Study Questions

1. What is the meaning of Jesus and Christ?
2. What was Peter's great confession at Caesarea Philippi?
3. What is the messianic secret?
4. What are the three basic types of Son of Man in the Synoptics?
5. How was Peter's response to Jesus (Mk 8:31-32) like that of the prosperity Gospel?
6. How did Jesus redefine the concept of Son of Man?
7. Why did the high priest think that Jesus spoke blasphemy (Mk 14:61-64)? Was it indeed blasphemy?

CHAPTER 5

THE MESSIANIC MISSION

The Synoptic Gospels devote a large amount of space to the suffering and death of Jesus. "The Gospel of Mark has often been described as a passion story with a long introduction."[1]

But while Paul has a detailed theology of the cross, the Synoptic Gospels offer a narrative history of the cross. So what is the significance of the cross for Jesus and the Synoptic writers?

The Necessity of Jesus' Death

Three times Jesus predicted his death (Mk 8:31; 9:31; 10:33). These predictions tell us that the death of Jesus was not an accident. It was the reason why he came.

In the first prediction Jesus says that "the Son of Man must (*dei*) suffer many things" (Mk 8:31). The Greek verb suggests that the death of Jesus was part of God's plan.

The second and third predictions also express the certainty of the future suffering and death of Jesus (Mk 9:31; 10:33).

After the third prediction of his death, Jesus said that "the Son of Man did not come to be served but to serve and give his life as a ransom

---

[1]G.E. Ladd, *A Theology of the New Testament*, p. 184.

for many" (Mk 10:45). This saying clearly states that Jesus came for a redemptive purpose. A ransom needed to be paid.

On a different occasion, Jesus asked James and John, "Can you drink the cup I drink or be baptized with the baptism I am baptized with?" (Mk 10:38). Elsewhere he said, "I have a baptism to undergo, and how distressed I am until it is completed" (Lk 12:50). This baptism was a reference to his death. Jesus knew that he had to die a violent death.

Earlier in his ministry Jesus said that "the time will come when the bridegroom will be taken from them" (Mk 2:20).

Jesus' death on the cross was not a historical accident. It was the reason why he came. It was at the heart of God's redemptive plan for the world. The amount of space given to the Passion Week in each of the Gospels is an indication of the theological importance of Jesus' death.

The Last Supper

At the end of his life, before his death, Jesus was very explicit about the significance of his death. The Last Supper pointed to the death of Jesus.

Mark tells us that on the night before he was betrayed, Jesus shared a final meal with his disciples. He broke the bread and said, "This is my body" (Mk 14:22). Then he took the cup and said, "This is my blood of the covenant, which is poured out for many" (Mk 14:24).

Matthew's Gospel includes the phrase, "for the forgiveness of sins." There Jesus said, "This is my blood of the covenant, which is poured out for many for the forgiveness of sins" (Mt 26:28).

In Luke we read, "This cup is the new covenant in my blood, which is poured out for you" (Lk 22:20). All three Gospels agree that the body and blood of Jesus was sacrificed for our sins.

All three Gospels also have an eschatological perspective. Jesus says, "I tell you the truth, I will not drink again of the fruit of the vine until that day when I drink it anew in the kingdom of God" (Mk 14:25).

The Meaning of The Cross

The Synoptic Gospels offer five basic perspectives on the death of Christ.[2]

First, Jesus' death is messianic. "The giving of his life is the objective for which Jesus came." His death is "the realization of the very purpose of his mission, the highest manifestation of his entire life of service to God and humanity."[3] Jesus came for the purpose of dying on the cross for humanity.

Second, the death of Jesus is atoning. This is especially clear in the word "ransom" (*lutron*) found in Mark 10:45 (cf. Mt 20:28). In the ancient world, a ransom was the price paid to redeem a slave or a prisoner of war. Jesus' death was "the price by which the forfeited lives of women and men might be reclaimed."[4] This price is paid to God, not to the devil. Paul in his theology develops the idea of ransom.

Third, Jesus' death is substitutionary. Jesus was punished in our place. Jesus' death was a ransom "for many" (Mk 10:45). He died as a substitute for us.

Fourth, Jesus' death was sacrificial. The statements at the Last Supper about "the blood of the covenant" make this clear. This phrase can be found in Exodus 24:8 at the institution of the Sinai covenant. The blood of sacrificed animals was called the blood of the covenant. Through this sacrifice Israel was brought into a covenant relation with

---

[2]See G.E. Ladd, *A Theology of the New Testament*, pp. 186-91.
[3]G.E. Ladd, *A Theology of the New Testament*, p. 187.
[4]G.E. Ladd, *A Theology of the New Testament*, p. 188.

God.[5] Jesus' sacrifice on the cross brings us into a similar covenant relation with God.

Finally, Jesus' death was eschatological. Jesus said that he would not drink again of the fruit of the vine until the future kingdom of God. "The death of Christ creates a new fellowship that will be fully realized only in the eschatological Kingdom of God."[6]

Although the Synoptics do not have a detailed theology of the cross, the basic elements of a theology of atonement are in place. Jesus died on the cross as a sacrifice for our sins so that we might live with him in the future kingdom of God.

The Resurrection of Jesus

In the Synoptic narratives, death does not have the final word. The Synoptic Gospels together with John and Paul testify to the fact that Jesus rose from the dead on Easter Sunday.

The resurrection of Jesus is an eschatological event. In the future, after we die, we will be raised again if we believe in Jesus. But now this eschatological event has occurred in history. It is an example of realized eschatology.

> The disciples must have experienced the appearances of the Risen Lord as an eschatological event, as a dawning of the turning point of the worlds.

The disciples saw these appearances of the risen Jesus as "the dawn of the time of salvation."[7]

The resurrection from the dead by Jesus was a guarantee of our resurrection into the future kingdom of God.

---

[5]See T. Palmer, *A Theology of the Old Testament*, pp. 64-65
[6]G.E. Ladd, *A Theology of the New Testament*, p. 191.
[7]J. Jeremias, *New Testament Theology*, p. 309.

But the resurrection of Jesus was also the beginning of his kingly reign. This idea is developed by Paul but is suggested especially by Matthew and Luke. At the end of Matthew's Gospel, Jesus said, "All authority in heaven and on earth has been given to me" (Mt 28:18). Luke's Gospel concludes with the ascension of Jesus into heaven (Lk 24:50-51). Jesus' kingly reign began with his resurrection and his ascension.

The disciples experienced Jesus' resurrection,

> As the dawn of the eschaton. They saw Jesus in shining light. They were witnesses of his entry into glory. In other words, they experienced the parousia.
>
> —J. Jeremias, *New Testament Theology*, p. 310.

The eschatological kingdom of God had already come in human history.

Study Questions

1. Was the death of Jesus on the cross a historical accident? Why or why not?
2. Why was it necessary for the Son of Man to suffer many things (Mk 8:31)?
3. Jesus said that his death was a ransom (Mk 10:45). What is a ransom? To whom was the ransom of Jesus paid?
4. Explain how the cup at the Lord's Supper is the blood of the covenant.
5. How is Jesus' death sacrificial and substitutionary?
6. How is the resurrection of Jesus an eschatological event?

CHAPTER 6

LIFE IN THE KINGDOM

Jesus is the promised Messiah who came to usher in the eschatological kingdom of God. Jesus came to call people to get ready for this kingdom. He came to form a new community of disciples who belong to the reign of God.[1]

So what is the life in the kingdom of God? How does one enter the kingdom of God?

Repentance

The Synoptic Gospels open with a call for repentance. Since the eschatological kingdom of God is near, repentance is imperative as a preparation for this kingdom. Both John and Jesus called on the people to repent since the kingdom of God is near (Mk 1:15; Mt 3:2, 4:17).

But it grieved Jesus that many of his own people refused to repent. He spoke woes to the towns in Galilee which did not repent while pagan cities like Tyre and Sidon would have repented (Mt 11:20-21). Even Nineveh repented at the preaching of Jonah (Mt 12:41).

The great example of a repentant sinner is the prodigal son. In the parable this son came to his senses and confessed his sins (Lk 15:21).

---

[1] J. Jeremias said: "the *only* significance of the whole of Jesus' activity is to gather the eschatological people of God" (*New Testament Theology*, p. 170).

"Repentance means learning to say *Abba* again, putting one's whole trust in the heavenly Father, returning to the Father's house and the Father's arms."[2]

Repentance means being sorry for one's sin and turning from one's sin. Zacchaeus, for example, repented and promised to restore that which was stolen (Lk 19:8).

Repentance is becoming like a child. "Whoever humbles himself like this child is the greatest in the kingdom of heaven" (Mt 18:4). Repentance is putting one's self in a child's relationship to his father. "The repentance of the lost son consists in his finding his way home to his father. In the last resort, repentance is simply trusting in the grace of God."[3]

Believing and Following Jesus

After announcing the kingdom, Jesus called people to follow him. He found the first four disciples and told them to follow him (Mk 1:14-20). Then he said to Levi, "Follow me" (Mk 2:14). The rich young ruler was also told to follow Jesus (Mk 10:21).

The Synoptic narratives record large crowds following Jesus (e.g., Mk 3:7; 5:24). Bartimaeus after being healed followed Jesus (Mk 10:52). During the passion of Jesus, Peter and the women continued to follow him (Mk 14:54; 15:41).

Entry into the kingdom is directly connected with the person of Jesus. A citizen of the kingdom will follow Jesus and believe in him.

The Synoptic Gospels offer examples of persons with faith. At times these persons stood at the fringe of Jewish society. Often the religious leaders were unbelieving, and even the disciples were of little faith.

---

[2]J. Jeremias, *New Testament Theology*, p. 156.
[3]J. Jeremias, *New Testament Theology*, p. 156.

A poor woman who suffered from bleeding was healed by Jesus, who told her, "Your faith has saved you" (Mk 5:34). Jesus spoke the same words to blind Bartimaeus after he was healed (Mk 10:52).

A Gentile centurion believed that Jesus could heal his paralyzed servant. Jesus said, "I have not found anyone in Israel with such great faith" (Mt 8:10/Lk 7:9). A Canaanite woman insisted that Jesus heal her demon-possessed daughter. Jesus remarked, "Woman, you have great faith" (Mt 15:28).

A sinful woman once anointed Jesus' feet with perfume as a sign of her faith. Jesus told her that her sins were forgiven and that her faith had saved her (Lk 7:48-50). But Simon the Pharisee was unbelieving.

Jesus called his generation "faithless" (Mk 9:19). Even the disciples and Peter were at times men "of little faith" (Mt 8:26; 14:31).

The Synoptic Gospels do not use the words "faith" and "believe" as often as Paul. But

> Jesus' whole message is one single summons to accept the offer of salvation, one single appeal to trust in his word and in God's grace; that is, it is a call to faith, even if that word does not occur very often.
>
> —J. Jeremias, *New Testament Theology*, p. 165.

Kingdom Ethics

Ethics in the kingdom of God are radical. Jesus spells them out after the first prediction of his death: "If anyone would come after me, he must deny himself and take up his cross and follow me" (Mk 8:34).

Self-denial contradicts the thinking of the world. Self-denial puts God and one's neighbor first. Self-denial "means the renunciation of one's own will so that the Kingdom of God may become the all-important concern of life."[4]

---

[4]G.E. Ladd, *A Theology of the New Testament*, p. 130.

The taking up of one's cross is similar in meaning. "The taking of the cross means the death of self, of personal ambition and self-centered purpose."[5]

Self-denial and bearing the cross are directly related to the great command of love. The summary of the law is the command to love God and one's neighbor (Mk 12:29-31).

This love (*agapē*) means service to one's neighbor. Our example is Jesus, "who did not come to be served but to serve and give his life as a ransom for many" (Mk 10:45).

Study Questions

1.   What is the meaning of repentance in the Synoptic Gospels?
2.   Give five examples of those who followed Jesus.
3.   Describe the faith of the tenth leper in Luke 17.
4.   Describe the faith of the centurion in Matthew 8.
5.   What is the meaning of self-denial and bearing the cross in Mark 8:34?

---

[5]G.E. Ladd, *A Theology of the New Testament*, p. 130.

CHAPTER 7

THE FUTURE KINGDOM

The paradox of the kingdom of God is that it is already present but not yet here. So what is Jesus' view of the future kingdom? When will the kingdom of God be fully realized?

The Return of Jesus

In the Synoptic Gospels, Jesus predicts his second coming. But when and how will Jesus come again? Three statements suggest that Jesus thought that his coming was imminent.

Once he said that "some who are standing here will not taste death before they see the kingdom of God come with power" (Mk 9:1). Perhaps the kingdom here is the glory of Jesus' resurrection or the event of Pentecost or the Transfiguration, all of which took place during the life of his disciples.

Again, Jesus said that his disciples "will not finish going through the cities of Israel before the Son of Man comes" (Mt 10:23). Perhaps this mission is the church's mission to the Jews which continues to this day.

Before his death Jesus said that "this generation will certainly not pass away until all these things have happened" (Mk 13:30). What are "all these things"? Perhaps they refer to the signs of the end which we continue to experience today.

The dominant message of the Synoptic Gospels in respect to his coming is: "No one knows about that day or hour, not even the angels in heaven, nor the Son, but only the Father" (Mk 13:32).

We do not know when Jesus will come again. But we are commanded to wait and watch. "Therefore keep watch because you do not know when the owner of the house will come back . . . . What I say to you, I say to everyone: 'Watch!'" (Mk 13:35-37).

Jesus describes the future in the Olivet Discourse (see Mk 13, Mt 24 and Lk 21). Before the second coming of Jesus, there will be signs of the end. There will be wars and rumors of war, earthquakes and famines. There will be false prophets and persecution. After these the end will come.

The second coming of Jesus will be loud and noisy. The sun and moon will be darkened, and the stars will fall from the sky.

> At that time people will see the Son of Man coming in clouds with great power and glory. And he will send his angels and gather his elect from the four winds, from the ends of the earth to the ends of the heavens.
>
> —Mk 13:26-27

The resurrection of the dead will then occur. Jesus expected the future "resurrection of the righteous" (Lk 14:14). In his discussion with the Sadducees, Jesus reaffirmed the belief in the resurrection of the dead, emphasizing that God "is not the God of the dead but of the living" (Mk 12:27).

Then the final judgment will occur. In Matthew 25 we have a picture of this future event. People will be judged on the basis of their faith which produces good works. Then the wicked "will go away to eternal punishment and the righteous to eternal life" (Mt 25:46).

Hades and Gehenna

At their death the unbelievers will go to Hades. Hades is the Greek equivalent of Sheol in the Old Testament. Hades is the place of the dead; but it is also a place of punishment.[1]

Capernaum would go down to Hades because of her unbelief (Mt 11:23/Lk 10:15). The gates of Hades would not prevail against the church (Mt 16:18). Again, Jesus depicted the rich man in torment in Hades (Lk 16:23).

The Greek word for hell is Gehenna (*geenna*). Usually hell is pictured as a place of fire. Jesus speaks of the "hell of fire" (Mt 5:22; 18:9). In hell the "worm does not die and the fire is not quenched" (Mk 9:47-48). Those who are unfaithful are "condemned to hell" (Mt 23:33).

But hell is also seen as outer darkness. Those who do not believe "will be thrown outside, into the darkness, where there will be weeping and gnashing of teeth" (Mt 8:12).

Thus the hot fire and the cold darkness are two metaphors for the final destiny of those who do not believe. But the essence of hell is "exclusion from the presence of God and the enjoyment of his blessings."[2]

Paradise and The Eternal Kingdom

Believers, on the other hand, will be with God. At his death Jesus said to the thief on the cross, "Today you will be with me in paradise" (Lk 23:43).

---

[1] J. Jeremias claims that Hades is the place of the ungodly during the intermediate state before the last judgment while Gehenna is the eternal place of judgment ("Geenna," in *Theological Dictionary of the New Testament* 1:658).

[2] G.E. Ladd, *A Theology of the New Testament*, p. 196.

Paradise is used in the Septuagint of the garden of Eden (Ezek 28:13; 31:8) but also of the messianic age. Paradise "simply designates the dwelling place of God."[3]

There are a few pictures or metaphors of the future kingdom. Once it is compared to "a feast with Abraham, Isaac and Jacob" (Mt 8:11). In Luke we have the image of being at Abraham's side (Lk 16:22).

At times the image of inheritance is used. Jesus will say to the righteous, "Come, you who are blessed by my Father; take your inheritance, the kingdom prepared for you since the creation of the world" (Mt 25:34).

Words will not be able to describe this future kingdom. For now, only metaphors will have to suffice. But the essence of the eternal kingdom is being with God and with Jesus.

Study Questions

1.   What is the essence of hell in the Synoptic Gospels?
2.   What is paradise in the Synoptic Gospels?
3.   Describe the future return of Jesus.
4.   What should be our response to the unknown time of Jesus' coming?
5.   What is the essence of the future kingdom?

---

[3]G.E. Ladd, *A Theology of the New Testament*, p. 195.

PART II

THE GOSPEL OF JOHN

The Gospel of John is significantly different than the Synoptic Gospels. In the Synoptics Jesus spoke often in parables; in John's Gospel Jesus gave longer theological speeches. The vocabulary of John is often different than that of the Synoptics. In the three Gospels "kingdom of God" and "kingdom of heaven" are found more than one hundred times; in John "kingdom of God" is found only four times. John's unique vocabulary includes life, light, darkness, love, truth, witness, believe and know.

It is generally believed that the Gospel of John was written a few decades after the Synoptic Gospels, probably at the end of the first century. John was writing in a Greek philosophical setting. Gnosticism was becoming a problem.

John's language is contextualized in the Greek context to refute Greek heresies. John uses Greek philosophical language to present Jesus. But the Gospel of John, who was an eye-witness, remains a reliable source of the teaching and works of Jesus.

CHAPTER 8

THE TWO WORLDS ON JOHN'S GOSPEL

The Synoptic Gospels, as we have seen, talk of two ages: the present evil age and the future age or the kingdom of God. A Christian is in both ages. If we understand time as a horizontal line, then this two-age structure could be called a horizontal dualism.

But John presents a vertical dualism.[1] There are two worlds—the world above and the world below. Jesus once said to the Jewish leaders: "You are from below; I am from above. You are of this world; I am not of this world" (Jn 8:23).

The world below is evil; the world above is good. This is a vertical dualism.

This World

The Greek word for "world" is *kosmos*. This word in John has three basic meanings.

Sometimes the world is the created physical world. Jesus speaks of the beginning or creation of the physical world (Jn 17:5,24). Jesus also speaks of the physical light of the world (Jn 11:9). This world

---

[1]See G.E. Ladd, *A Theology of the New Testament*, pp. 259-72.

is the created world that God made. This world was originally good. The Prologue proclaims of Jesus: "Through him all things were made; without him nothing was made that has been made" (Jn 1:3). This world was originally good.

Sometimes the world is all of humanity. Jesus claimed to have spoken openly to the world or all mankind (Jn 18:20). The Pharisees complained that "the whole world has gone after him" (Jn 12:19). The world is all the Jewish people and even the Gentiles. It is this world of humanity that God loves: "For God so loved the world that he gave his one and only Son" (Jn 3:16).

But often in John the world is those people in the world who live in enmity with God. Jesus said that "the world . . . hates me because I testify that what it does is evil" (Jn 7:7). Even though Jesus came into the world, "the world did not know him" (Jn 1:10). The world also does not know or love the Father (Jn 17:25).

The prince of this world is Satan. Before his death Jesus said that "the prince of this world is coming," but "he has no hold on me" (Jn 14:30). At Jesus' crucifixion, "the prince of this world will be driven out" (Jn 12:31).

This world is a world of darkness because of its sin. At the incarnation, "the light shines in the darkness, but the darkness has not understood it" (Jn 1:5). And, "light has come into the world, but people loved darkness instead of light" (Jn 3:19).

The disciples, then, were to be in the world but not of the sinful world (Jn 17:14,18).

The Heavenly World

The good news of John's Gospel is that light and life came down from the heavenly world.

After he fed the five thousand with bread, Jesus compared himself to the manna that came from heaven: "For the bread of God is he who comes down from heaven and gives life to the world" (Jn 6:33). Jesus said, "I am the living bread that came down from heaven. If anyone eats of this bread, he will live forever" (Jn 6:51).

Jesus told the Jewish leaders that "I am not of this world" (Jn 8:23). He told Pilate, "My kingdom is not of this world" (Jn 18:36).

Jesus is the one who came down from heaven to do the Father's will. He said, "I have come down from heaven not to do my will but to do the will of him who sent me" (Jn 6:38). He also said, "No one has ever gone into heaven except the one who came from heaven, the Son of Man" (Jn 3:13).

When his work was completed, he would return to heaven. Before his death, "Jesus knew that the time had come for him to leave this world and go to the Father" (Jn 13:1). After the resurrection Jesus told Mary and the disciples, "I am returning to my Father and your Father, to my God and your God" (Jn 20:17).

The heavenly world stands in contrast to the world below. This is the vertical dualism.

An Ethical Dualism?

According to some Greek philosophy and Gnosticism, this present world is bad because it is made of matter; but the heavenly world is good because it is spiritual or non-physical.

This is what we call a nature-grace dualism. The evil material world of nature stands in opposition to the good spiritual world of grace.

But the Gospel of John proclaims that the world of matter was originally not bad but good. Through the Logos, "all things were made;

without him nothing was made that has been made" (Jn 1:3). God the Word created this material world as something good.

The incarnation is a powerful reminder that the material world is not necessarily bad. At the incarnation, "the Word became flesh" (Jn 1:14). The divine Word from heaven actually took on human flesh (sarx).

In John's Gospel there is not a nature-grace dualism but rather an ethical or sin-grace dualism. The ethical dualism in John's Gospel is the opposition that exists between the world of sin and the world of grace.

The real problem in the world is sin, not physical matter. A basic principle is that "everyone who sins is a slave to sin" (Jn 8:34). When the Holy Spirit comes, "he will convict the world of guilt in regard to sin and righteousness and judgment" (Jn 16:8).

At the incarnation this world was a world of sin. The light shone in the darkness but the darkness did not understand it (Jn 1:5). Satan is the prince of this world. "He was a murderer from the beginning, not holding to the truth, for there is no truth in him" (Jn 8:44).

The evil principle of the world, then, is sin, not physical matter. The good principle is God and his grace. The good principle was manifest when the Word became flesh (Jn 1:14). This Word is the Lamb "who takes away the sin of the world" (Jn 1:29).

The basic dualism of John's Gospel is an ethical dualism. Jesus, who is the light, came to overcome the darkness.

Study Questions

1. Explain the vertical dualism found in John.
2. What are the three meanings of "world" in John?
3. Is the physical world good or bad for John? Why?
4. Does John agree with Greek dualism? Why or why not?
5. Describe the ethical dualism of John's Gospel.

CHAPTER 9

JOHANNINE CHRISTOLOGY

The Gospel of John was written so that we might believe "that Jesus is the Messiah, the Son of God" (Jn 20:31). So who is Jesus according to John's Gospel?

Messiah

The Greek word *Christos* is found about 20 times in this Gospel. Usually it is a title, meaning "messiah" or "anointed one." Twice *Messias* is found as a transliteration of the Hebrew "Messiah" (Jn 1:41; 4:25).

The Jewish people looked forward to the Messiah as the expected Davidic king. The Gospel of John announces that Jesus is this Messiah.

When Andrew met Jesus, he told his brother Simon, "We have found the Messiah!" (Jn 1:41). On meeting Jesus, Nathanael exclaimed, "Rabbi, you are the Son of God; you are the King of Israel" (Jn 1:49). The "King of Israel" is a reference to the Messiah.

The Samaritan woman expected the Messiah. Jesus told her, "I who speak to you am he" (Jn 4:25-26). Martha confessed, "I believe that you are the Messiah, the Son of God" (Jn 11:27).

At a critical point in the Gospel, Peter confessed that Jesus is "the Holy One of God" or the Messiah (Jn 6:69).

The purpose of John's Gospel, as we have seen, is to lead the reader to the belief that Jesus is the Messiah (Jn 20:31).

Son of Man

The title "Son of Man" is used only by Jesus of himself, as in the Synoptic Gospels. But the title is used less frequently in John.

Usually this title is used in connection with the work of Jesus, especially his suffering and death. To Nicodemus, Jesus said that "the Son of Man must be lifted up" as the snake was lifted up in the wilderness (Jn 3:14).

In a similar way, Jesus said, "The hour has come for the Son of Man to be glorified" (Jn 12:23). But the crowd was puzzled. They asked, "How can you say, 'The Son of Man must be lifted up?' Who is this 'Son of Man'?" (Jn 12:34). Like the disciples in Mark 8, this crowd could not understand how the Son of Man or the Messiah could suffer. But it is this same Son of Man who also has the authority to judge on the final day (Jn 5:27).

We are challenged like the blind man with the question, "Do you believe in the Son of Man?" (Jn 9:35). The blind man who was healed said, "Lord, I believe" and he worshiped Jesus (Jn 9:38).

Son of God

The main christological idea in John is that of sonship. The purpose of the Gospel is to demonstrate that Jesus is not only the Messiah but also the Son of God (Jn 20:31).

Jesus speaks of God as his Father more than one hundred times in this Gospel. (In Mark's Gospel Jesus calls God his Father only four times.)

> It is obvious that Jesus' sonship is the central christological idea
> in John, and that he writes his Gospel to make explicit what is
> implicit in the Synoptics.
>
> —G.E. Ladd, *A Theology of the New Testament*, p. 283.

There is a special and close relationship between the Father and the Son. Six dimensions of this relationship can be mentioned.[1]

First, the Son was sent by the Father into the world. Jesus said,

> God so loved the world that he gave his one and only Son . . . .
> God did not send his Son into the world to condemn the world
> but to save the world through him.
>
> —Jn 3:16-17

Second, the Son is the special object of the Father's love. "The Father loves the Son and shows him all he does" (Jn 5:20).

Third, the Son's works are the Father's works. "The Son can do nothing by himself . . . whatever the Father does the Son also does" (Jn 5:19).

Fourth, the Son's words are also the Father's words. Jesus said, "I do nothing on my own but speak just what the Father has taught me" (Jn 8:28).

Fifth, the Son claims to have exclusive knowledge of the Father. "No one has seen the Father except the one who is from God; only he has seen the Father" (Jn 6:46). In the high-priestly prayer, Jesus says to the Father, "though the world does not know you, I know you" (Jn 17:25).

This leads us to the final point: there is a unity between the Father and the Son. Jesus said, "I and the Father are one . . . the Father is in me,

---

[1]See G. E. Ladd, *A Theology of the New Testament*, pp. 284-85. Complete Scripture references can be found there.

and I in the Father" (Jn 10:30,38). Again, he said, "I am in the Father, and the Father is in me" (Jn 14:11).

Jesus' prayer for his disciples is that "they may be one as we are one" (Jn 17:11). He prays to the Father "that all of them may be one just as you are in me and I am in you" (Jn 17:21).

This is the profound testimony of the Gospel of John. There is a very close relationship between the Father and the Son. These statements point to the divinity of Jesus.

The Logos

These statements are in accord with the majestic prologue of John's Gospel:

> In the beginning was the Word, and the Word was with God,
> and the Word was God. He was with God in the beginning.
>
> —Jn 1:1-2

The Greek word *logos* can be translated as "word" or "speech." Jesus is the speech of God.

The first verse of John reminds us of the Old Testament and especially the first verse of Genesis. The word (*dabar*) of God is prominent in the Old Testament.

But *logos* was also a meaningful term in the Greek philosophical world. The *logos* for the Greeks was often a rational principle of the world.

John took this pregnant term and applied it to Jesus. Jesus is the Word that reveals God. Since the Word was close to the Father, the Word is able to reveal God.

A Divine Savior

John's Gospel offers a clear testimony to the divine nature of Jesus. The Gospel opens by confessing that "the Word was God." This Word created the world (Jn 1:1-3).

During one dialogue, the Jewish leaders tried to kill Jesus because he was "making himself equal with God" (Jn 5:18). At another time, when Jesus said that he and the Father are one, the religious leaders again tried to kill him "for blasphemy, because you, a mere man, claim to be God" (Jn 10:33).

Jesus claimed that "before Abraham was born, I am" (Jn 8:58-59). At the end of the Gospel, Thomas confessed, "My Lord and my God" (Jn 20:28).

But this Word is also fully human. In the Prologue, we are told that "the Word became flesh" (Jn 1:14). His flesh was his real humanity.

Jesus is pictured as fully human in his ministry on earth. He enjoyed a wedding feast with his mother (Jn 2:1-11). He wept at the death of a friend (Jn 11:35). He was troubled at the thought of death (Jn 12:27).

In the middle of a hot day, Jesus was tired and thirsty (Jn 4:6-7). On the cross he cried, "I thirst" (Jn 19:28).

In his teaching, Jesus also used metaphors to describe himself. These "I am" sayings tell us that Jesus is also the Savior.

Jesus is the bread of life (Jn 6:35) and the light of the world (Jn 8:12; 9:5). He is both the gate for the sheep (Jn 10:7) and the good shepherd (Jn 10:11,14). He is also the true vine (Jn 15:1).

Jesus is also "the resurrection and the life" (Jn 11:25) and "the way and the truth and the life" (Jn 14:6).

This divine-human Word of God is our Savior.

Study Questions

1. What do Christos and Son of Man tells us about Jesus?
2. How was the Son of Man glorified according to John 12:23?
3. Describe the special relationship between the Father and the Son in John 17.
4. Why is it significant that Jesus is God's Word?
5. How is Jesus the bread of life according to John 6?
6. How is Jesus a vine to the branches in John 15?

CHAPTER 10

ETERNAL LIFE

The problems facing humanity in the Gospel of John are sin and death. The coming of Jesus provides salvation from sin and death.

Salvation From Sin

Jesus came to take away our sins and to defeat evil. This happened on the cross.

When John the Baptist saw Jesus, he said, "Behold, the Lamb of God who takes away the sin of the world" (Jn 1:29). The lamb here is a sacrificial lamb as found in the Old Testament. The death of Jesus on the cross was the means by which our sins are removed.

Jesus told Nicodemus that the Son of Man must be lifted up like the serpent in the wilderness. This is a reference to Jesus' death on the cross. The lifting up of Jesus will give eternal life to those who believe in him (Jn 3:14-15).

Once Jesus said, "Unless you eat the flesh of the Son of Man and drink his blood, you have no life in you" (Jn 6:53). The eating and drinking of Jesus point to his death on the cross which is commemorated in the Lord's Supper. It is this sacrifice on the cross that gives life.

John's narrative of the crucifixion of Jesus at the Passover time suggests that Jesus is the Passover lamb who died for us. The quotation from the Passover story in Exodus about the bones of the lamb not being broken supports this (Jn 19:36).

At the cross and the resurrection, Satan was defeated. Just before his death, Jesus said, "Now is the time for judgment on the world; now the prince of this world will be driven out" (Jn 12:31). Right before his crucifixion, Jesus said, "I have overcome the world" (Jn 16:33).

In a way not fully developed, the death of Jesus provides liberation from sin and evil.

Believing And Knowing

So how does one receive eternal life? John is absolutely clear: through faith.

The Greek noun for faith, *pistis*, is absent from John's Gospel. But the verb, *pisteuō*, occurs about one hundred times. *Pisteuō* means "to have faith" or "to believe."

The purpose of the Gospel, as we have seen, is so that the reader might "believe that Jesus is the Messiah, the Son of God, and that by believing may have life in his name" (Jn 20:31).

The object of the faith is usually Jesus. But faith in Jesus and faith in God are the same. Once Jesus said, "Believe in God; believe also in me" (Jn 14:1).

Believing in God is the same as knowing God. John defines eternal life as knowing God and Jesus Christ. "This is eternal life—that they may know you, the only true God, and Jesus Christ, whom you have sent" (Jn 17:3).

Knowing God is the same as loving God. Knowing in the Old Testament is often a deep and personal knowledge, which is love. (In

Genesis 4:1, for example, Adam knew his wife and they had a son).
Faith brings a person into a personal relationship of love with God.

This relationship is also expressed by the verb "to abide" or "to
remain" (*maneō*). Jesus tells a believer to "abide in me and I will abide
in you. . . . If a person abides in me and I in him, he will bear much
fruit" (Jn 15:4-5). The vine and the branches are an illustration of this
personal relationship.

This relationship is explained elsewhere. Jesus said that when the
Holy Spirit comes,

> you will know that I am in my Father, and you are in me, and
> I am in you. May they also be in us.
>
> —Jn 14:20

Our fellowship on earth should mirror that in heaven. Jesus prays
"that all of them will be one, Father, just as you are in me and I am in
you" (Jn 17:21).

Love and obedience are evidence of abiding in Jesus. Jesus said, "If
anyone loves me, he will obey my teaching. . . . He who does not love
me will not obey my teaching" (Jn 14:23).

Jesus also said, "A new commandment I gave you: Love one
another. As I have loved you, so you must love one another" (Jn
13:34-35).

The model of love is Jesus himself:

> My command is this: Love each other as I have loved you.
> Greater love has no one than this, that one lay down his life
> for his friends.
>
> —Jn 15:!2

Eternal Life

A person who believes and loves God will have eternal life. Eternal life is a future, eschatological concept. In the future, if we believe, we will have eternal life.

Jesus said,

> For my Father's will is that everyone who looks to the Son and believes in him shall have eternal life, and I will raise him up at the last day.
>
> —Jn 6:40

This is a future reality.

Jesus also said, "I am the resurrection and the life. He who believes in me will live, even though he dies" (Jn 11:25). Again, eternal life is a future reality.

But this future eschatological reality is now present for the believer. "Whoever believes in the Son *has* eternal life" (Jn 3:36). The tense is present.

Jesus also said,

> Whoever hears my word and believes him who sent me *has* eternal life and will not be condemned; he has crossed over from death to life.
>
> —Jn 5:24

Already we are now enjoying eternal life.

Eternal life is both a present and a future reality. Jesus said, "Whoever eats my flesh and drinks my blood *has* eternal life, and I will raise him up at the last day" (Jn 6:54). We see here that this eternal life is both present and future.

The Holy Spirit

Integral to the Christian life is the Holy Spirit. John's Gospel has a deep theology of the Holy Spirit.

In some sense, the Holy Spirit is the cause of one's faith. Jesus said, "Unless a person is born of water and the Spirit, he cannot enter the kingdom of God" (Jn 3:5). Jesus compares the work of the Spirit to the blowing of the wind. "The wind blows wherever it pleases. . . . So it is with everyone born of the Spirit" (Jn 3:8).

The Spirit is active in the believer. The Spirit is compared to "streams of living water" that flow within a believer (Jn 7:38-39).

At the end of the Gospel, the coming Spirit is called the Counselor or the "Paraclete" (*paraklētos*). The Paraclete will come after Jesus leaves. He will continue the work of Jesus.

The Paraclete will teach the believers truth. Jesus said that the Counselor "will teach you all things and will remind you of everything I have said to you" (Jn 14:26). He is "the Spirit of truth" who will testify about Jesus (Jn 15:26).

The Paraclete will also speak the truth to the world: "when he comes he will convict the world of guilt in regard to sin and righteousness and judgment" (Jn 16:8).

But the Holy Spirit will also live within a believer. After Jesus leaves, the Counselor will be with us forever. We shall know him "for he lives with you and will be in you" (Jn 14:17).

Eternal life then is life in the Spirit. It is believing in Jesus and having eternal life. Eternal life is not just a future reality: eternal life is knowing or loving God and Jesus Christ and having the Holy Spirit in us.

Study Questions

1. How is Jesus the Passover lamb according John 1 and John 19?
2. When will Satan be defeated according to John 12:31-33?
3. What is eternal life according to John 17:3?
4. What is the importance of abiding in Christ according to John 15?
5. What are the tasks of the Paraclete (Counselor or Comforter) in John 14-16?

PART III

THE EARLY CHURCH

The book of Acts is our primary source for the life of the early church in its first few decades. The book of Acts contains an account of the growth of the early church. It also contains records of some of the first sermons by Peter and Paul especially.

Of course Acts was written by Luke and reflects his theology as well. But it is our assumption that the book of Acts is a reliable historical record of both these first events and first speeches.

At the crucifixion all of the disciples except John had run away. At the end of Mark's Gospel, the women fled from the tomb, saying nothing to anyone "because they were afraid" (Mk 16:8). But at the beginning of the book of Acts, the apostles were fearlessly preaching the Gospel.

Obviously something dramatic had happened. The book of Acts presupposes the resurrection and ascension of Jesus. It was the eschatological resurrection of Jesus in human time which changed everything.

CHAPTER 11

THE EARLY CHURCH'S KERYGMA

The book of Acts contains the story of the remarkable growth of the Christian church at its beginning. The church grew partly through the testimony of individual believers; but it was also the public preaching of apostles that led to this growth.

The Greek work for preaching is *kērugma*. What was the kerygma of the early church? One scholar suggests six main points of this preaching.[1]

First, "the age of fulfillment has dawned." What happened in the death and resurrection of Jesus was a fulfillment of Old Testament prophecies (e.g., Acts 3:18,24).

Second, this took place through the ministry, death and resurrection of Jesus. The sermons in Acts focus especially on Jesus' death and resurrection (e.g., Acts 2:23-24).

Third, Jesus was exalted to God's right hand and he exercises authority from heaven (e.g., Acts 2:33-36).

Fourth, the Holy Spirit is the sign of Christ's present power and glory (e.g., Acts 2:33).

---

[1] C.H. Dodd, *The Apostolic Preaching and Its Developments* (1936), pp. 38-45; cited by G.E. Ladd, *A Theology of the New Testament*, p. 365.

Fifth, the messianic age will reach its consummation in the return of Jesus (e.g., Acts 3:21).

Sixth, the kerygma always carries an appeal for repentance, the forgiveness of sins and the Holy Spirit (e.g., Acts 2:38-39).

The heart of the early apostolic preaching was the death and resurrection of Jesus. These two events changed the history of the world.

The Suffering of Jesus

The suffering and death of Jesus are central to the apostolic kerygma. So what is the significance of Jesus' death? The book of Acts does not have a developed theology of the atonement. But there are indications of its significance.

Peter in his sermon at Pentecost said that Jesus was handed over "by God's set purpose and knowledge" (Acts 2:23). Later, Peter said that the leaders in Jerusalem "did what [God's] power and will had decided beforehand should happen" (Acts 4:27-28).

In another sermon Peter said that in the crucifixion "God fulfilled what he had foretold through all the prophets, saying that his Messiah would suffer" (Acts 3:18). Jesus' death was part of God's redemptive plan.

A unique title for Jesus in Acts is God's servant. Four times the Greek word *pais* (servant) is used of Jesus. In a prayer to God the believers spoke of the suffering of "your holy servant Jesus" (Acts 4:27,30). But Peter in one of his sermons spoke of glorifying "his servant Jesus" and raising "his servant" (Acts 3:13,26).

The believers in Acts saw Jesus as being both the suffering servant of Isaiah and the glorious Messiah expected by the Jews. Thus we have a "conflation of the roles of Servant and Messiah."[2]

---

[2]G.E. Ladd, *A Theology of the New Testament*, p. 367.

Often in Acts Jesus is called the *Messiah*. Christos in Acts is usually a title, not a proper name. Jesus is the Messiah prophesied in the Old Testament. He suffered as the Messiah; now he is the exalted Messiah.

The Exaltation of Jesus

In the kerygma of the early church in the book of Acts, the exaltation of Jesus seems to be more prominent than the suffering of Jesus. In other words, there is a theology of glory as well as a theology of cross in the early preaching.

Peter's sermon at Pentecost illustrates this. Only one verse (Acts 2:23) describes the crucifixion of Jesus. But thirteen verses (Acts 2:24-36) describe his exaltation.

Quoting Psalm 16, Peter proclaimed that Jesus was not abandoned in the grave but was raised again to life. After his resurrection, Jesus was exalted to the right hand of God. Peter concludes: "God has made this Jesus, whom you crucified, both Lord and Messiah" (Acts 2:36).

In Acts "the resurrection stands as the heart of the early Christian message."[3] The criterion of a new apostle is that he be a witness of the resurrection. The disciples chose Matthias who was "a witness with us of [Jesus'] resurrection" (Acts 1:22).

The main point of Peter's sermon after the healing of the crippled man was that God "glorified his servant Jesus" (Acts 3:13). This is also the essence of Peter's message to the Sanhedrin: "The God of our fathers raised Jesus from the dead . . . . God exalted him to his own right hand as Prince and Savior" (Acts 5:30-31).

The resurrection is also prominent in Paul's preaching. The main emphasis of Paul's sermon at Antioch in Pisidia is the resurrection of Jesus (Acts 13:30-37). In Athens, Paul was preaching "the good news about Jesus and his resurrection" (Acts 17:18). At his trial before Felix,

---

[3]G.E. Ladd, *A Theology of the New Testament*, p. 353.

Paul said, "It is concerning the resurrection of the dead that I am on trial before you today" (Acts 24:21).

The exaltation of Jesus is a prominent theme in the early preaching of the church in the book of Acts.

Jesus is Lord

The exaltation of Jesus means that he is Lord. This is a common title for Jesus in the book of Acts.

At the end of his Pentecost sermon, Peter said that God made Jesus "Lord and Messiah" (Acts 2:36). This lordship is a result of Jesus' resurrection and ascension.

But was not Jesus Lord before the resurrection? As God, Jesus was always Lord. But now within salvation history Jesus has become Lord in a special way. Now he is ruling with the Father in heaven at the Father's right hand.

The first confession of the early church was "Jesus is Lord" (Rom 10:9). "The heart of the early Christian confession is the Lordship of Christ."[4]

If Jesus is Lord, then repentance is the only proper response. When Peter concluded his Pentecost sermon, the audience wanted to know what to do. Peter said, "Repent and be baptized" (Acts 2:38). The conclusion of Paul's sermon at Antioch in Pisidia is also a call for faith in Jesus which leads to justification (Acts 13:38-39).

The preaching of the early church is consistent: Jesus died and rose from the dead; therefore one should repent and believe.

---

[4]G.E. Ladd, *A Theology of the New Testament*, p. 375.

Study Questions

1.   What is the significance of the death of Jesus in the book of Acts?
2.   How does the title "servant of God" clarify the idea of Jesus' messiahship?
3.   Does Acts have a theology of glory or a theology of the cross? Explain.
4.   How did Jesus become Lord in Acts 2:36?
5.   What is the significance of Jesus' lordship for us Christians?

CHAPTER 12

THE HOLY SPIRIT AND THE CHURCH

The book of Acts contains the story of the Holy Spirit and the early church. Before his death Jesus predicted the coming of the Spirit. The Spirit continues the work of Jesus.

The Holy Spirit

The book of Acts begins with the expectation of the Holy Spirit. Jesus before his ascension told the disciples to stay in Jerusalem to "wait for the promise of the Father" (Acts 1:4). This promise is the Holy Spirit.

On Pentecost day the Holy Spirit came upon the disciples. There was a sound of a strong wind, tongues of fire and the speaking in tongues.

In his sermon Peter explained what was happening. Peter quoted from Joel's prophecy of the day of the Lord. This was an eschatological prophecy. Referring to Joel, Peter said that "in the last days" God would pour out his Spirit on all people (Acts 2:17).

This suggests that the pouring of the Spirit, like the kingdom of God and eternal life, is an eschatological event. With Pentecost "the last days have come . . . the messianic era has come, the eschatological salvation is present."[1]

And yet the day of the Lord is still a future event at the end of time. This is the already-not yet dynamics of Acts. "The time of fulfillment has come; but the Day of the Lord remains an eschatological event in the indeterminate future."[2] The kingdom is already but not yet present.

Baptism of The Holy Spirit

At the beginning of the book Jesus told the disciples that "in a few days you will be baptized with the Holy Spirit" (Acts 1:5).

The phrase "baptize with (or, 'in') the Holy Spirit" occurs only seven times in the New Testament. In Mark's Gospel, John the Baptist says, "I will baptize you with water, but [Jesus] will baptize you with the Holy Spirit" (Mk 1:8). John's Gospel is similar (Jn 1:33). In Matthew and Luke, Jesus "will baptize with the Holy Spirit and fire" (Mt 3:11; Lk 3:16).

So when would Jesus baptize with the Holy Spirit? Clearly this took place after Jesus' ascension on the day of Pentecost. Before his ascension, Jesus had said that in a few days his disciples would be baptized with the Holy Spirit. The initial baptism with the Holy Spirit occurred with the believers at Pentecost.

After Pentecost, Peter was called to the house of Cornelius. While Peter was speaking to Cornelius and his family, "the Holy Spirit came on all who heard the message" (Acts 10:44). Peter later interpreted this as a baptism of the Holy Spirit (Acts 11:15-16).

Some Christians think that baptism in the Holy Spirit is a second blessing reserved for only some believers. But the New Testament

---

[1]G.E. Ladd, *A Theology of the New Testament*, p. 381.
[2]G.E. Ladd, *A Theology of the New Testament*, p. 381.

suggests that this baptism occurs at the beginning of the Christian life of every believer.

This is clear in Paul's first letter to the Corinthians. The church in Corinth had a lot of problems—factions, sexual immorality, idolatry and the like. Yet Paul said that "we were *all* baptized by one Spirit into one body . . . and we were *all* given the one Spirit to drink" (1 Cor 12:13; italics added).

Baptism in the Holy Spirit is analogous to conversion. When we believe, we are baptized by the Holy Spirit. This happened at the beginning of the church at Pentecost; this happened at the conversion of Cornelius; and it still happens today.

It should be noted that baptism in the Holy Spirit and water baptism are not the same. When a person believes, he or she is baptized by the Holy Spirit. Later this Spirit baptism is confirmed by water baptism.

Filled With The Holy Spirit

Baptism in the Holy Spirit occurs at the beginning of the Christian life. During the Christian life, a believer should strive to be filled with the Holy Spirit.

Two men in Acts were said to be "full of the Holy Spirit." Stephen, who was chosen to be one of the seven, was "full of faith and of the Holy Spirit" (Acts 6:5). At his martyrdom he was still "full of the Holy Spirit" (Acts 7:55).

Barnabas was also "full of the Holy Spirit and faith" (Acts 11:24). A person who is full of the Holy Spirit is one who is under the dominant influence of the Holy Spirit. This is a spiritual condition.

But at critical times in the history of the early church, the Holy Spirit filled men and women. At Pentecost the disciples were filled with the Holy Spirit and began to speak in tongues (Acts 2:4). Later Peter, standing in front of the Sanhedrin, was filled with the Spirit and spoke boldly (Acts 4:8).

On another occasion the believers were together and they were filled with the Holy Spirit and spoke the word of God boldly (Acts 4:31). Paul was once filled with the Holy Spirit and confronted the sorcerer Elymas (Acts 13:9).

Persons filled with the Holy Spirit will do a variety of things in the service of God. In Acts some spoke in tongues and others spoke boldly. Speaking in tongues is not the only manifestation of the filling of the Holy Spirit.

In his letter to Ephesus, Paul commanded every believer: "Be filled with the Spirit" (Eph 5:18). The verb, which in Greek is a present imperative, suggests continual action. Our entire lives should continually be under the influence of the Holy Spirit.

The Church

The Christian church began at Pentecost. Of course God had his elect people throughout the Old Testament. But the Christian church is defined by the presence of the Holy Spirit and by Christian baptism.

The Greek word for "church" is *ekklēsia*. *Ekklēsia* in Greek is a gathering of citizens or an assembly. The *ekklēsia* of God or of Christ are those who believe in Jesus and who are baptized with water.

Often in Acts the *ekklēsia* is the local church. The book of Acts talks of the church in Antioch and the churches in Syria and Cilicia (Acts 11:26; 13:1; 15:41).

But at least once the *ekklēsia* is the universal church. At Miletus, Paul talked of "the church of God, which he bought with his own blood" (Acts 20:28).

Water baptism is the rite of initiation into the church. Christian baptism, as Matthew tells us, is baptism "in the name of the Father and of the Son and of the Holy Spirit" (Mt 28:19). Christian baptism is being "buried with [Christ] through baptism into death" (Rom 6:4).

John's baptism was a pre-Christian baptism. The believers in Ephesus who were baptized with John's baptism had not yet received Christian baptism. They received Christian baptism and the Holy Spirit when Paul preached to them (Acts 19:4-7).

The earliest officers of the church were the apostles. They had special authority because they were with Jesus. The office of apostle ceased when the apostles died. The other main early church office is that of elder or overseer.

At the council of Jerusalem, the leaders of the church were the apostles and elders (Acts 15:2,4,6). When Paul was going to Jerusalem, he called the elders of Ephesus to meet him at Miletus (Acts 20:17).

An elder (*presbuteros*) is the same as a bishop or overseer (*episkopos*). At Miletus, Paul told the elders that God had made them overseers over the church (Acts 20:28). Elder and overseer are two names for the first regular office of the church.

The early church was characterized by a deep fellowship (*koinōnia*). Most of the first churches were house churches. Believers met together in private homes to worship and fellowship with each other. The early believers reflected Christ's love.

Study Questions

1. Read Acts 2:16-21. Why would the outpouring of the Holy Spirit be seen as an eschatological event?
2. What do you think baptism in the Holy Spirit is?
3. What is evidence that a person is filled with the Holy Spirit?
4. Why is John's baptism not a Christian baptism?
5. Describe the relation between water baptism and Spirit baptism.
6. Read Acts 20:25-31. What are the responsibilities of the elder or overseer?

PART IV

THE THEOLOGY OF PAUL

The greatest mind in the New Testament to interpret the meaning of the person and work of Jesus is the converted Pharisee, Paul.
> —G.E. Ladd, *A Theology of the New Testament*, p. 398.

Paul wrote thirteen of the New Testament books. Most or all of Paul's letters were actually written before the four Gospels.

"Paul was a man of three worlds: Jewish, Hellenistic and Christian."[3] Paul was

> Circumcised on the eighth day, of the people of Israel, of the tribe of Benjamin, a Hebrew of Hebrews; in regard to the law, a Pharisee.
>> —Phil 3:5

His letters reflect a deep acquaintance with the Old Testament scriptures.

Paul was well at home in the Greek world. He was fluent in the Greek language and culture. He was born in the city of Tarsus, which was a Roman city.

---

[3]G.E. Ladd, *A Theology of the New Testament*, p. 398.

But a life-changing event occurred on the road to Damascus. Jesus appeared to Paul and his life was totally changed. Paul became a Christian. For Paul all things became new.

CHAPTER 13

THE PRESENT EVIL AGE IN PAUL

There are two ages in Paul's theology. The old, evil age stands in contrast to the new kingdom of God.

This Evil Age and this World

The present evil age (*aiōn*) is the present world of sin. Jesus came and "gave himself for our sins to rescue us from the present evil age" (Gal 1:4).

The "god" of this age is Satan. Paul says, "The god of this age has blinded the minds of unbelievers" (2 Cor 4:4). The rulers of this age are under Satan. It was "the rulers of this age" who "crucified the Lord of glory" (1 Cor 2:8). These rulers were Herod, Pilate and the Jewish religious leaders.

This age has its own secular philosophy. Paul asks, "Where is the philosopher of this age?" (1 Cor 1:20). The wisdom of God transcends the philosophy of this age.

A Christian is not to be "conformed to this age" (Rom 12:2). In the past before their conversion, the believers in Ephesus once "followed the ways of this age" (Eph 2:2). But now they belong to the kingdom of God.

The kingdom of God stands in contrast to this present evil age.

The word *kosmos* or "world" is often synonymous with *aiōn* or age. Sometimes *kosmos* denotes the universe, the inhabited earth or humanity in general. But frequently the *kosmos* is fallen humanity that lives in rebellion against God.

Paul equates the philosophy of this age with the wisdom of this world. The "wisdom of the world" is contrasted with "the wisdom of God" (1 Cor 1:20-21). The "wisdom of this world," he says, "is foolishness in God's sight" (1 Cor 3:19).

The "spirit of the world" is also contrasted with the Spirit of God (1 Cor 2:12-14). Formerly, Paul says, "we were in slavery under the basic principles of the world" (Gal 4:3). But for a Christian "the world has been crucified" (Gal 6:14).

This world, like this age, "usually means the human situation qualified by sin." It is "the world turned away from God, rebellious and hostile toward him."[1]

Principalities And Powers

This evil world is full of evil spirits. Their leader is Satan. Satan, who is the god of this age, is "the ruler of the kingdom of the air" (Eph 2:2).

He is called "the devil" and "the evil one" in the passage on the armor of God (Eph 6:11,16). But "the God of peace will crush Satan under your feet" (Rom 16:20).

Under Satan are principalities and powers. These spiritual powers were originally created by Christ: "In him all things were created . . . whether thrones or powers or rulers or authorities" (Col 1:16). But at some point they rebelled against God.

Today,

---

[1]H. Ridderbos, *Paul*, p. 92.

> Our struggle is not against flesh and blood but against the
> rulers, the authorities, the powers of this dark world and the
> spiritual forces of evil in the heavenly realms.
>
> —Eph 6:12

But Christ "disarmed the powers and authorities" on the cross (Col
2:15). He ascended "far above all rule and authority and power and
dominion" (Eph 1:21). Therefore Paul is convinced that angels and
principalities will not separate us from Christ (Rom 8:38-39).

Paul, like the African, believes in the reality of evil spiritual
powers.

Flesh

A unique Pauline term to describe one's sinful nature is *sarx* or "flesh."
There are three different senses of *sarx*.[2]

Sometimes "flesh" refers to the physical body. Paul tells the
Colossian believers that he is absent from them "in the flesh" (Col 2:5).
Here the flesh is the human body.

At times "flesh" refers to humanity. When Paul encountered Jesus,
he did not consult "with flesh and blood" (Gal 1:16). "Flesh and blood"
refers to other people.

But usually in Paul *sarx* or flesh is man's sinful nature. (Some
translations translate *sarx* as "sinful nature.")

In Romans 8, flesh (*sarx*) and spirit (*pneuma*) are two opposing
principles.

> The mind of the flesh is death; but the mind of the Spirit is life
> and peace because the mind of the flesh is hostile to God. It does
> not submit to God's law, nor can it do so. Those that are in the
> flesh cannot please God.
>
> —Rom 8:6-8

---

[2]H. Ridderbos, *Paul*, p. 94.

In this passage, flesh is bad, and the Spirit is good.

In Galatians, the works of the flesh are sexual immorality, idolatry, hatred and the like; but the fruit of the Spirit include love, joy and peace (Gal 5:19-23). Again, the flesh is bad and the Spirit is good.

This is the so-called ethical use of flesh. "Flesh is thus a description of sin itself, in the most inclusive sense of the word."[3] It is obvious from Paul that the problem with humans is not their physical body but their spiritual nature.

The ethical dualism of Paul is the dualism between the flesh or the sinful human nature on the on hand and the Spirit of God on the other hand. The flesh as sinful human nature is evil; the Spirit of God is good.

The Essence of Sin

The basic problem of humanity is sin. Paul stresses the universality of sin: "there is no one righteous, not even one; there is no one who understands, no one who seeks God" (Rom 3:10-11). Paul continues: "all have sinned and fall short of the glory of God" (Rom 3:23).

Paul describes the sinful life of the unbelieving pagans in the Roman Empire:

> They are darkened in their understanding and separated from the life of God . . . . Having lost all sensitivity, they have given themselves over to sensuality so as to indulge in every kind of impurity, with a continual lust for more.
>
> —Eph 4:18-19

In the first chapter of Romans, Paul describes the depravity that people sank to when they suppressed the creational knowledge of God. Such people fell into idolatry when they "exchanged the glory of the immortal God for images made to look like mortal man and birds and

---

[3]H. Ridderbos, *Paul*, p. 103; see G.E. Ladd, *A Theology of the New Testament*, pp. 511-17.

animals and reptiles" (Rom 1:23). Such people also "have become filled with every kind of wickedness, evil, greed and depravity" (Rom 1:29).

Sin is a pollution of our created nature. But the essence of sin is rebellion against God: "Sin in its essence is rebellion against God, refusal to be subject to him, enmity against God, disobedience."[4]

Paul tells the Colossians that "once you were alienated from God and were enemies in your minds because of your evil behavior" (Col 1:21).

Sin consists of enmity with God and our own pollution.

The Wrath of God

A basic consequence of our sin is the wrath of God. The first chapter of Romans says, "The wrath of God is being revealed from heaven against all the godlessness and wickedness of men" (Rom 1:18).

The wrath of God is his response to sin. "Wrath expresses what God is doing and what he will do with sin."[5] "God's wrath is altogether determined by his righteousness and holiness."[6]

God's wrath against sin is a present reality. In the above text, the wrath of God "is being revealed" (Rom 1:18). But his wrath is also a future reality. At the last judgment God's wrath will be revealed. Paul tells the wicked that "you are storing up wrath against yourself for the day of God's wrath when his righteous judgment will be revealed" (Rom 2:5).

A result of sin is alienation between us and God. Paul tells the Ephesians that once they were "separate from Christ . . . without God" and "far away" (Eph 2:12-13).

---

[4]H. Ridderbos, *Paul*, p. 105.
[5]G.E. Ladd, *A Theology of the New Testament*, p. 447.
[6]H. Ridderbos, *Paul*, p. 109.

One is reminded of the African myth of the woman who when pounding her yams struck God, who then retreated back to heaven. This is a picture of the human situation before the coming of Christ. We offended God and he was far from us.

Study Questions

1. Describe this present evil age.
2. Describe the origin and destiny of the principalities and powers.
3. What is the "flesh" in Galatians 5:19-21?
4. What is the essence of sin according to Paul?
5. How can the love of God and the wrath of God both be true?

CHAPTER 14

PAULINE CHRISTOLOGY

The power of the evil age is strong. But "when the fullness of time had come, God sent his Son" to redeem us (Gal 4:4). A new age, predicted in the Old Testament, had come.

Paul says that the mystery that was kept hidden for generations has finally been revealed. Paul was an evangelist of "the mystery that has been kept hidden for ages . . . but is now disclosed to the saints" (Col 1:26). The mystery of God is "Christ, in whom are hidden all the treasures of wisdom and knowledge" (Col 2:2-3).

The appearance of Jesus occurred in "the fullness of time" (Gal 4:4). Paul's language echoes that of Jesus: "The time is fulfilled . . . the kingdom of God is near" (Mk 1:15). There is a realized eschatological dimension to the first coming of Jesus.

"The whole content of the mystery that has now been revealed can be qualified and summarized in the one word— Christ."[1] So who is this Christ?

Christ

During Jesus' life, *Christos* was a title meaning "the Messiah." Jesus was the expected Messiah. But in Paul Christos is now a personal name

---

[1] H. Ridderbos, *Paul*, p. 49.

for Jesus. Paul calls him "Jesus Christ" eighty times and "Christ Jesus" eighty-nine times.[2]

The name "Christ" reminds us that Jesus is indeed the Messiah. Jesus is the one promised by the prophets, "who was descended from David according to the flesh" (Rom 1:2-3).

Jesus is fulfillment of Isaiah's prophecy of "the root of Jesse" who will spring up and rule over the nations (Rom 15:12). Jesus Christ is the one who was raised from the dead and "descended from David" (2 Tim 2:8).

In Africa, personal names have significance. The significance of the name "Christ" is clear—Jesus is the promised Messiah who came in the fullness of time.

Son of God

Jesus is indeed the Messiah. But a decisive Pauline concept is that of Son of God.

At his resurrection, Jesus was declared to be the Son of God. Paul says that Jesus was "declared with power to be the Son of God by his resurrection from the dead" (Rom 1:4). This was a public proclamation of the new authority that Jesus received at his resurrection.

But Jesus was Son of God even before his birth. Paul assumes the pre-existent sonship of Christ. Already before his birth in Bethlehem, Christ was the Son of God.

When Paul speaks of God sending his Son, this presupposes that the Son existed before the incarnation. In the fullness of time "God sent his Son" (Gal 4:4).

God was "sending his own Son in the likeness of sinful flesh" (Rom 8:3). Again, God "did not spare his own Son but gave him up for us all" (Rom 8:32).

---

[2]T. Schreiner, *New Testament Theology*, p. 319.

The Son then existed before the incarnation. This pre-existent Son was also divine. Paul teaches the divinity of Christ in a few key passages.

In his letter to the Philippians, Paul tells us that Jesus was in "the form of God" and had "equality with God" (Phil 2:6). This is a striking affirmation of Christ's divinity.

The letter to the Colossians also suggests Jesus' divinity. Jesus is "the image of the invisible God" and "the firstborn of all creation." He is also the agent of the creation of the world (Col 1:15-17).

The term "firstborn" does not mean that Jesus was born in time. Instead it conveys Jesus' authority over creation. David in Psalm 89:27 is called God's firstborn, "the most exalted of the kings of the earth," despite the fact that he was not Jesse's firstborn child.

Jesus is "the image of God" (2 Cor 4:4; cf Col 1:15). This term suggests a close relationship between God the Father and Jesus.

A couple of times, Jesus is explicitly called God. In Romans, Christ is "God over all, forever praised" (Rom 9:5). Elsewhere Paul calls Jesus "our great God and Savior" (Titus 2:13).

Paul is convinced that Jesus Christ was God. Jesus existed in heaven before his incarnation. Jesus was the agent of creation. In time God sent his Son into the world for our redemption.

The Humanity of Jesus

Paul also assumes the full humanity of Jesus. The great hymn in Philippians proclaims that Jesus, who existed in the form of God, "emptied himself" and "took the form of a servant, being made in human likeness." He was found "in appearance as a man" (Phil 2:7-8).

(When Jesus emptied himself, he did not lose his divinity. Instead, he gained the humble form of our humanity).

We read elsewhere that Jesus was "born of a woman, born under the law" (Gal 4:4). "According to the flesh," Jesus "was born of the seed of David" (Rom 1:3).

Although he was not present, Paul reports what he was told that "the Lord Jesus, on the night he was betrayed, took bread . . . and broke it" (1 Cor 11:23-26).

Paul was told about "the meekness and gentleness of Christ" (2 Cor 10:1). Paul also knew that "Christ did not please himself" but instead suffered insults (Rom 15:2-3).

There is no doubt that Paul believed in the full humanity of Jesus during his life on earth.

Jesus is Lord

The earliest confession of the church was "Jesus is Lord" (Rom 10:9). The Roman emperor was not lord in an absolute sense; instead, Jesus is the supreme Lord.

Paul says that no one can say "Jesus is Lord" except by the Holy Spirit (1 Cor 12:3). Paul says that he preaches "Jesus Christ as Lord" (2 Cor 4:5).

In a real sense, Jesus was Lord from eternity. Paul confesses that there is only "one Lord, Jesus Christ, through whom all things came and through whom we live" (1 Cor 8:6).

But Jesus became Lord in a special way after his death and resurrection: "Christ died and returned to life so that he might be the Lord of both the dead and the living" (Rom 14:9).

After Jesus' suffering, God highly exalted him so that "every knee should bow . . . and every tongue confess that Jesus Christ is Lord" (Phil 2:9-11).

At his resurrection and ascension, Christ was seated,

> Far above all rule and authority, power and dominion . . . God placed all things under his feet and appointed him to be head over everything for the church.
>
> —Eph 1:21-22

Christ is now reigning "until he has put all his enemies under his feet" (1 Cor 15:25).

Even though Christ was Lord from eternity, he assumed the special office of Lord at his resurrection and ascension.

The lordship of Christ means that we are servants or slaves to Jesus. Paul calls himself "a slave of Christ Jesus" (Rom 1:1). Every believer is "a slave of Christ" (1 Cor 7:22).

It is our duty to serve our Lord. Paul reminds the Colossian slaves that "it is the Lord Christ you are serving" (Col 3:24).

Jesus Christ for Paul is the pre-existent Son who was sent by God to redeem us. Jesus is now Lord over everything. We should serve this Lord.

Study Questions

1. What does Philippians 2:6-8 teach us about the person of Christ?
2. What does Colossians 1:15-17 teach us about the person of Christ?
3. Why is it important that Jesus be both divine and human?
4. What was the earliest confession of the Christian church?
5. According to Romans 1:1-4, when did Jesus become Lord?
6. What does it mean for you that Jesus is Lord?

CHAPTER 15

THE BLOOD OF JESUS

The death of Jesus on the cross is a central part of Paul's message. Paul said that "the word of the cross . . . is the power of God" (1 Cor 1:18).

Paul uses a number of metaphors to explain the meaning of the cross. We will consider some of these metaphors.

Propitiation

This key term is used only once in Paul. In Romans Paul says that God presented Jesus as a "propitiation through faith in his blood" (Rom 3:25). The Greek word is *hilasterion*. Some translations wrongly translate this word as "expiation," which is a sacrifice that takes away sins. But the correct translation is "propitiation."[1]

African readers are more familiar with the idea of propitiation than Europeans. In African traditional religion, sacrifices of propitiation were made to appease the gods or to turn away their wrath. In the same way, the death of Jesus was a sacrifice to turn away the wrath of God the Father.

The book of Romans shows two sides of the nature of God. First, because God is holy his wrath is revealed against all godlessness (Rom

---

[1]See L. Morris, *The Apostolic Preaching of the Cross*, pp. 167-72.

1:18). A sacrificial payment is necessary to satisfy the holy justice of God.

But, remarkably, it is also God in his love who provides the solution. In Romans 3:25, it is God himself who provides Jesus as a sacrifice to satisfy God's own just wrath. God's holiness is the problem; God's love is the solution.

Jesus' death is a propitiation for the wrath of God. When Jesus paid for our sins, the wrath of God was turned away from us.

The Blood of Christ

In five key texts Paul talks of the blood of Jesus. He says that there is propitiation through faith in his blood (Rom 3:25); we are justified by his blood (Rom 5:9); there is redemption through his blood (Eph 1:7); we are brought near through his blood (Eph 2:13); and there is peace through the blood of the cross (Col 1:20).

So what is the blood of Jesus in Paul? Many people assume that the actual blood of Jesus has magical powers. They would then cover their houses or cars with the blood of Jesus.

But the background to the blood of Jesus is the Old Testament sacrificial system. The blood of the sacrificial animal is the means of atonement. Leviticus tells us that "it is the blood that makes atonement for one's life" (Lev 17:11).

Christ is the lamb that was sacrificed for us. Paul writes: "For Christ, our Passover lamb, has been sacrificed" (1 Cor 5:7). This reminds us of John the Baptist's testimony that Jesus is the lamb that takes away the sins of the world (Jn 1:29).

> The idea of shed blood refers to the slaughter of the sacrificial
> lamb, whose throat was cut and whose blood gushed forth. . . .

In the New Testament, blood means life violently taken away,
life offered in sacrifice.
—G.E. Ladd, *A Theology of the New Testament*, p. 467.

We are justified by the sacrifice of Jesus; we are redeemed through his sacrifice; we have propitiation through this sacrifice; and we have peace or reconciliation because of the sacrifice.

The blood of Jesus in Paul's writings is not a magical potion; instead it is the sacrifice of Christ that pays for our sins.

Redemption

Another metaphor for the death of Jesus is that of purchasing or ransoming. These are metaphors from the marketplace.

Every Roman or Greek town had a marketplace. This market was called an *agora*. The word *agorazō* means to buy something, often in a marketplace. Paul uses this word to refer to our redemption. The English word "to redeem" means "to buy."

Paul tells the Corinthian believers that "you were bought with a price" (1 Cor 6:20; 7:23). So what was the price? The price was the death of Jesus on the cross.

A cognate word is *exagorazō*. Paul says that Christ came "to redeem those under law" (Gal 4:5). Also, "Christ redeemed us from the curse of the law by becoming a curse for us" (Gal 3:13).

Redemption is the process of buying a person or persons. Jesus redeemed us by paying a price. The price was his death on the cross.

Another concept from the marketplace is ransom. (The Greek word for ransom is *lutron*.) A ransom price is the money that was spent to free a slave.

We have seen from the Gospels that the Son of Man gave his life as a ransom for many (Mk 10:45). Paul uses the same metaphor to describe our salvation.

A basic word for redemption is *apolutrōsis*, which is the buying back or freeing of a slave. Paul speaks of the "redemption that is in Christ Jesus" (Rom 3:24). In Christ "we have our redemption through his blood" (Eph 1:7; cf Col 1:14).

These terms suggest the fact that Jesus paid a price to free us from our slavery. Jesus' death is the ransom price for our liberty.

Justification

Another metaphor to describe the work of Christ is a legal metaphor, namely, justification. The context is the court of law.

Before God's court of law, we are all guilty. We are all unjust and guilty. Therefore, we are all under the curse of the law. We all deserve punishment.

But Paul proclaims the good news of the righteousness of God. In the Gospel "a righteousness of God is revealed" (Rom 1:17; cf Rom 3:21). What is this justice or righteousness?

The righteousness of God is the amazing possibility of our justification or acquittal. We are declared just or righteous because of the sacrifice of Jesus on the cross.

Paul says that "since we have now been justified by [Christ's] blood, how much more shall we be saved from God's wrath through him" (Rom 5:9).

In this passage, the blood or sacrifice of Christ is the ground of our justification. We are made just because of Christ's sacrifice.

The same idea is found in Romans 3. All have sinned and "are justified freely by [God's] grace through the redemption that is in Christ Jesus" (Rom 3:24).

Again, the ground of our justification is the redemption or propitiatory sacrifice of Jesus. We are declared righteous because of what Jesus did on the cross.

So what happened on the cross? Paul says in Galatians that everyone who does not fully obey the law is cursed (Gal 3:10). But "Christ redeemed us from the curse of the law by becoming a curse for us" (Gal 3:13).

Our justification consists of Jesus taking the curse on himself that belongs to us. The result is that Jesus was cursed on the cross so that we might be free from the curse. In this way, we are acquitted and justified.

In another place, Paul said that "God made him who had no sin to be sin for us so that in him we might become the righteousness of God" (2 Cor 5:21). Jesus was our substitute on the cross.

The result of this process of justification is that both God and the believer are righteous. We see this in Romans 3. God did this

> To demonstrate his justice at the present time, so as to be just
> and the one who justifies the one who has faith in Jesus.
> —Rom 3:25-26

In the end, God is just because the just demands of the law have been satisfied. Believers are also just or acquitted before the law because their sins have been paid for.

Reconciliation

A final metaphor describing the work of Christ is reconciliation. This is a metaphor from the world of social relations.

Once "we were God's enemies" (Rom 5:10). This is because of our sins and hostility to God. But the death of Christ brought reconciliation.

Paul says that "when we were God's enemies, we were reconciled to him through the death of his Son." Through Jesus "we have now received reconciliation" (Rom 5:10-11).

Again, the death of Jesus is decisive. Christ's death is the ground of our salvation. Christ's death effected a change of relations with

God. We are now no longer God's enemies but his friends. This is because Jesus' death was a propitiation to turn away God's wrath. This happened when Jesus paid for our sins.

The process of reconciliation is explained in the second letter to the Corinthians: "God was reconciling the world to himself, not counting people's sins against them" (2 Cor 5:19).

Reconciliation—like justification—occurs when our sins are not counted against us. Our sins are not counted against us because Jesus became a curse for us (Gal 3:13). It was Jesus who satisfied the demands of the law.

Conclusion

The death of Jesus on the cross is central in Paul's theology. The sacrifice of Jesus changed things. God's justice was satisfied when Jesus bore our sins.

The price that Jesus paid was great—it was his own life. Jesus redeemed and ransomed us through his death. He purchased us through his blood.

Jesus' death was a propitiation that turned away God's wrath. God's wrath was turned away when his justice was satisfied.

The result is our acquittal or justification before God's law. The result is also our reconciliation. We are no longer enemies with God but friends. We now have peace through the blood of Jesus.

Study Questions

1. How is the death of Christ a propitiation?
2. "My car is covered by the blood of Jesus." Evaluate this statement from Paul's theology of the cross.
3. Explain the meaning of ransom and redemption in the context of our salvation.
4. Explain how we become righteous through justification.
5. Describe the process of reconciliation in 2 Corinthians 5:18-21.

CHAPTER 16

LIFE IN CHRIST

Christ's death and resurrection offer us the possibility of a radically new life. What was Paul's view of this new life?

In Christ

A vital phrase in Paul's theology is the "in Christ" formula. The phrases *en Christō* (in Christ) or *en autō* (in him) or the like are found about 164 times in Paul's letters.[1] Our entire Christian life is grounded in the person and work of Jesus Christ.

Our election is in Christ: God "chose us in him before the foundation of the world" (Eph 1:4). Our justification is in Christ (Gal 2:17). Our redemption "is in Christ Jesus" (Rom 3:24). Our sanctification is in Christ: the believers at Corinth were "sanctified in Christ Jesus" (1 Cor 1:2).

Our salvation "is in Christ Jesus" (2 Tim 2:10). Our reconciliation is in Christ: "God was reconciling the world to himself in Christ" (2 Cor 5:19). And, "now in Christ Jesus you who once were far away have been brought near though the blood of Christ" (Eph 2:13).

---

[1] L. Smedes, *All Things Made New*, p. 78.

To a certain extent, the "in Christ" formula denotes "the Christian's relation to the eschatological saving event."[2] Our entire salvation is grounded in Christ.

But at a deeper level, the person who is in Christ is in a deep personal relationship with Jesus. Paul says that "if anyone is in Christ, he is a new creation" (2 Cor 5:17).

Paul tells the Colossian believers that "you died and your life is now hidden with Christ in God" (Col 3:3). An intimate relation between Christ and the believer is suggested here.

Paul considers everything to be loss so that he may gain Christ "and be found in him" (Phil 3:8-9). Paul is also convinced that "there is now no condemnation for those who are in Christ Jesus" (Rom 8:1). Therefore, nothing will "separate us from the love of God that is in Christ Jesus our Lord" (Rom 8:38-39).

One commentator says: "The life of faith is one of living union and communion with the exalted and ever-present Redeemer."[3]

If we believe in Jesus, we are in Christ. But Christ is also in us. Paul says of his conversion: "I have been crucified with Christ and I no longer live but Christ lives in me" (Gal 2:20).

It is by faith that Christ lives in us. Paul prays for the Ephesians "that Christ may dwell in your hearts through faith" (Eph 3:17).

But where Christ is, the Holy Spirit is also present. Paul once said that "the Lord is the Spirit" (2 Cor 3:17).

Paul tells the Roman believers that "the Spirit of God lives in you" and "Christ is in you" (Rom 8:9-10). The two realities belong together.

A believer receives the Spirit not through the works of the law but through faith (Gal 3:2). The Holy Spirit lives in the one who has faith.

---

[2] W. Kümmel, *The Theology of the New Testament*, p. 219.
[3] J. Murray, *Redemption—Accomplished and Applied*, p. 209.

A believer is like a temple in which God lives: "Don't you know that you yourselves are God's temple and that God's Spirit lives in you?" (1 Cor 3:16).

A Christian is one who is in Christ and in whom Christ and his Spirit live.

Dying And Rising With Christ

Paul describes the Christian life in terms of dying and rising with Christ. In a sense this is metaphorical language since we were not present in Jerusalem when Jesus died and rose two thousand years ago. Yet this language expresses in a deep way the Christian life.

When a person believes in Jesus, he or she has died with Christ. In Romans 6, Paul says that the believers "died with Christ" (Rom 6:8). In Colossians it is again affirmed that "you died with Christ" (Col 2:20). The Greek tense in both places is aorist, which is a past, completed action.

Dying with Christ is the decisive event when our sins are put to death. Dying with Christ occurs at the time of conversion or initial faith. We die with Christ when we believe in him and are justified by faith. Dying with Christ "denotes the same reality as being justified by faith."[4]

At the time of conversion, a believer also is raised with Christ. Paul tells the Colossian believers that "you were . . . raised with him through your faith in the power of God" (Col 2:12). Again, Paul says that "you have been raised with Christ" (Col 3:1).

The Greek tense in these two places is the aorist tense, signifying again a past completed action. We were raised with Christ when we received new life from the Holy Spirit.

------

[4]W. Kümmel, *The Theology of the New Testament*, p. 207.

Yet there is a paradox in Paul's theology. Already we died and rose with Christ. Yet we must continue to put to death the earthly nature and to put on the Christian life.

This is the dialectic of the indicative and the imperative. The indicative is the statement of fact: already we died and rose with Christ. The imperative is the command: continue to put to death your earthly nature and to put on the Christian life.

We see this paradox in Colossians. Already we died and rose with Jesus (Col 2:20; 3:1). But we must continue to put to death that which is earthly and to put on Christian life (Col 3:5,12).

As in the Synoptic Gospels, the believer is part of two worlds. The eschatological kingdom of God is already present in our lives: already we have eternal life. Already we are justified. But the old sinful aeon is still present and requires sanctification.

Study Questions

1. What does Paul mean in 2 Corinthians 5:17 when he says that we are in Christ?
2. What does Paul mean when he says that "the Lord is Spirit" (2 Cor 3:17)?
3. What does Paul mean when he says in Romans 6 that we died with Christ?
4. What does Paul mean when he says in Romans 6 that we were raised with Christ?
5. Describe the indicative and imperative in the Christian life.

CHAPTER 17

RIGHTEOUSNESS AND HOLINESS

The basic human problem is our guilt and unrighteousness. But God sent his Son into the world so that we might become righteous. What kind of righteousness then do we receive from Jesus Christ?

Justification as Acquittal

Paul says that no one is righteous (*dikaios*) (Rom 3:10). But God's righteousness (*dikaiosunē*) has been revealed (Rom 3:21). His righteousness consists in believers being justified or made righteous (Rom 3:24). (The Greek word for "to justify" is *dikaioō*.)

So how are we justified or made just? Is justification a change in our behavior or is justification a change in our legal status?

Paul is clear on this issue. Repeatedly we are told that justification is not by our doing the works of the law but only by faith. Justification is not something that we ourselves do; justification is a legal declaration that we are not guilty.

On the one hand, Paul repeatedly tells us that we are not made just or righteous by our own actions: "no one will be justified by the works of the law" (Rom 3:20); "a person is justified by faith apart from the works of the law" (Rom 3:28);

> A person is not justified by the works of the law but through
> faith in Jesus Christ . . . no one will be justified by the works
> of the law
>
> —Gal 2:16

"No one is justified by the law before God" (Gal 3:11).

On the other hand, Paul is equally clear that we are justified or made just by faith. The righteousness of God is "from faith unto faith," for "the righteous shall live by faith" (Rom 1:17). The righteousness of God is a righteousness "through faith in Jesus Christ" (Rom 3:22). "A person is justified by faith apart from the works of the law" (Rom 3:28).

> A person is not justified by the works of the law but through
> faith in Jesus Christ . . . even we believed on Christ Jesus that
> we might be justified by faith in Christ.
>
> —Gal 2:16

It is thus clear that justification is a legal declaration of righteousness and not a change in one's behavior. In other words, justification is a forensic or legal declaration of righteousness.

The context of justification is the future judgment seat. In the eschaton (end of time), we will be judged according to our faith and our deeds. Justification then is an eschatological concept.

Looking to the future, Paul asks, "Who will bring any charge against those whom God has chosen?" The answer is that no one can bring a charge against them since "it is God who justifies" (Rom 8:33).

Elsewhere, Paul speaks of "the hope of righteousness" (Gal 5:5). Justification is a future, eschatological reality.

But justification is also an accomplished fact for the believer. Already, "we have been justified by faith" and "we have peace with God" (Rom 5:1). Already, "we have been justified by [Christ's] blood" (Rom 5:9). Already, "you were washed, you were sanctified, you were justified" (1 Cor 6:11).

Again, we see the "already"-"not-yet" dynamic of the Christian faith. Our salvation is already present and yet future.

The great example of the justified person is Abraham. "Abraham believed God, and it was credited to him as righteousness" (Rom 4:3). Paul clearly states that Abraham was not justified by works (Rom 4:2). Instead, he was justified by faith. Abraham "is the father of all who believe" (Rom 4:11).

The result of the process of justification is that the believer is just (*dikaios*). He or she is no longer under the wrath of God. Because the believer is just, he or she now has peace with God (Rom 5:1).

But this justice or righteousness is a legal, forensic justice. Where is the justice or righteousness in our lives?

Sanctification as Holiness

A related term to justification is sanctification. Justification means "making just." Sanctification means "making holy." They are similar in meaning.

(In Greek, "just" or "righteous" is *dikaios*; holy is *hagios*. "To justify" is *dikaioō*; "to sanctify" is *hagiazō*.)

Paul uses sanctify in two ways. Sometimes sanctify means to consecrate or set apart; at other times, it means to make holy.

Sometimes sanctification means to consecrate or make holy in a ceremonial or ritual way. It is related to the Old Testament idea of setting apart. For example, Paul tells Timothy that created things are good because they are "sanctified by the word of God and prayer" (1 Tim 4:4-5).

In a similar way, the believers in Corinth were "sanctified in Christ Jesus" (1 Cor 1:2) even though they were not very holy. Here, sanctification is close in meaning to justification. The believers were made holy when they believed in Jesus and were justified.

Again, Paul calls Jesus "our righteousness, holiness and redemption" (1 Cor 1:30). All three of these terms refer to our justification. We are righteous, holy and redeemed because Jesus paid for our sins.

In these cases, sanctification is synonymous with justification. But in other cases, sanctification or holiness refers to the process of becoming holy in our personal lives.

Holiness (*hagiasmos*) is an important idea in the first letter to the Thessalonians. Holiness should be the goal of the Christian life.

Paul told the Thessalonians that God's will is their sanctification or holiness (1 Thess 4:3). They should control their bodies "in holiness and honor" (1 Thess 4:4). God did not call us for impurity "but in holiness" (1 Thess 4:7). Paul's final prayer for them is: "May God . . . sanctify you through and through" (1 Thess 5:23).

The purpose of our election is holiness. God "chose us in [Christ] before the creation of the world to be holy and blameless in his sight" (Eph 1:4).

Our entire lives should be lives of holiness. We should offer our bodies as living sacrifices, "holy and pleasing to God" (Rom 12:1).

Jesus' goal is to present his church "as a radiant church, without stain or wrinkle or any other blemish, but holy and blameless" (Eph 5:27).

Holiness (*hagiasmos*) is similar in meaning to righteousness (*dikaiosune*). Those who died with Christ and were justified should live a life of righteousness. They should be "slaves of righteousness" (Rom 6:18). They should offer their bodies "in slavery to righteousness leading to holiness" (Rom 6:19).

There is then a fundamental harmony between justification and sanctification. The concern of both is righteousness and holiness.

The initial problem is that we were not just or righteous. Through faith we were justified or made righteous before the law. Through the Holy Spirit our lives are made righteous and holy.

Justification is the legal statement of our righteousness. Sanctification in the second use of the term is the practical holiness and righteousness in our lives.

Justification is the indicative (the statement of fact): we are righteous! Sanctification in its second use is the imperative (the command): be holy or righteous!

Both justification and sanctification are possible because through faith we are in Christ.

Study Questions

1. How can a person become just or righteous?
2. Define justification.
3. Explain the two meanings of sanctification.
4. In 1 Corinthians 1:2, how are the Corinthian Christians both holy and not holy?
5. Describe the place of good works in justification and sanctification.
6. Are you a saint? Why or why not?

CHAPTER 18

THE CHURCH IN PAUL

A Christian does not live in isolation. A believer is part of a community called the *ekklēsia* or the church. What does Paul say about the church?

The Body of Christ

Paul uses different images to describe the church. One of the most prominent is that of body. The body illustrates the unity and the diversity of the church.

The human body has many different members: the eye, the ear, the foot and the hand, for example. Each member has a different function. In the same way, the church as the body of Christ has different members. Every member has its own gifts or functions.

The image of the body emphasizes the diversity of the church: "We have different gifts according to the grace given us" (Rom 12:6). But the unity of the church is also stressed: "If one part suffers, every part suffers with it; if one part is honored, every part rejoices with it" (1 Cor 12:26).

In Romans and First Corinthians, the church is the entire body of Christ. But the metaphor changes in Ephesians and Colossians. There Christ is the head, and the church is the rest of the body.

These latter two epistles stress the authority of the head over the rest of the body. In a general way, Jesus' authority as head is "over everything" (Eph 1:22). But in a special way, Jesus is head over the church. Paul writes: "For the husband is the head of the wife as Christ is the head of the church, his body, of which he is the Savior" (Eph 5:23).

There is an intimate connection between the head and the body. Paul writes in a pre-scientific way when he says that it is the head "from whom the whole body, supported and held together by its ligaments and sinews, grows as God causes it to grow" (Col 2:19). Paul here emphasizes that the life of the church comes from Jesus Christ, who is the head.

The image of the body reminds us of the unity that we as diverse believers have. It also reminds us of the authority of Jesus over the church.

A Holy Building

A second metaphor for the church is that of a building or a temple. This image also emphasizes the unity of Christians.

Paul tells the believers in Corinth: "you are God's building" (1 Cor 3:9). Just as a building is made of many stones, the church is made of many believers. Paul continues by observing that Jesus Christ is the foundation of the building (1 Cor 3:11). Paul and the other evangelists are the builders. The building materials must be reliable lest they be burned with fire.

But the metaphor then changes. Paul then calls the Corinthian believers a temple of God (1 Cor 3:16-17). This new image speaks of the holiness expected of the church. But there is also a promise: "God's Spirit lives in you" (1 Cor 3:16). God's Spirit causes the temple to be holy.

The letter to the Ephesians has the same imagery. The Ephesian church is built on the foundation of the apostles and prophets with Jesus as the chief cornerstone. In Christ the temple becomes a holy temple filled with the Holy Spirit (Eph 2:19-22).

These related metaphors teach us the unity and the holiness of the church. We are reminded of the apostolic nature of the church. A church must also be in intimate union with Jesus Christ and the Holy Spirit.

Baptism And The Lord's Supper

The rite of initiation into the church is water baptism. In Corinth Paul baptized Crispus, Gaius and the household of Stephanas (1 Cor 3:14-16).

Baptism "represents identification of the believer with Christ."[1] The believers in Galatia "were baptized into Christ." They were also clothed with Christ (Gal 3:27).

Baptism is an identification of the believer with the death of Jesus: "Don't you know that all of us who were baptized into Christ Jesus were baptized into his death?" (Rom 6:3). Baptism is a picture of our dying with Christ.

The Lord's Supper is also a reminder of the death of Christ for the believer. Paul tells the Corinthian believers that the cup is "a participation in the blood of Christ" and the bread is "a participation in the body of Christ" (1 Cor 10:16). Through faith a person participates in the death of Christ. The Lord's Supper is a reminder of this participation.

The Lord's Supper is also a symbol of the love and unity of the church. Paul writes: "Because there is one loaf, we who are many are one body for we all partake of the one loaf" (1 Cor 10:17).

---

[1] G.E. Ladd, *A Theology of the New Testament*, p. 593.

Paul also insists that when the church comes together to celebrate the Lord's Supper, they must do so in a spirit of love. Paul deplores the divisions and the chaos in the Corinthian celebration of the ceremony. He concludes that "it is not the Lord's Supper you eat" (1 Cor 11:20).

The Lord's Supper should be a testimony of our oneness with Christ and our oneness with one another.

Church Administration

The *ekklēsia* for Paul is both the universal church and the local one.

Sometimes the *ekklēsia* is the universal church. In Ephesians and Colossians, as we have seen, Jesus is the head of the church (e.g., Eph 5:23; Col 1:18). This is the universal church.

But often *ekklēsia* refers to the church in one place. Paul speaks of "the church in Cenchrea" (Rom 16:1); "the church of the Laodiceans" (Col 4:16); and "the churches" in Galatia and Judea (Gal 1:2,22). These are local churches.

There are also house churches in Paul's epistles. A church or fellowship met in the house of Philemon (Phm 1:2); a church met in the house of Aquila and Priscilla (1 Cor 16:19; Rom 16:3-5); there was also a church in the house of Nympha (Col 4:15).

At the beginning, in the book of Acts, it was the apostles who governed the church, especially in Jerusalem. But as the church spread throughout the Roman Empire, local church government developed in different places.

Paul tells the believers in Thessalonica to respect "those who work hard among you, who are over you in the Lord and who admonish you" (1 Thess 5:12). Those who are over the believers are the leaders of the church. Probably these leaders were the elders.

We have seen from the book of Acts that an elder (*presbuteros*) is the same as an overseer (*episkopos*). In his first letter to Timothy,

Paul writes, "The elders who direct the affairs of the church well are worthy of double honor, especially those whose work is preaching and teaching" (1 Tim 5:17).

This verse suggests two categories of elders: governing elders and teaching ones. All the elders are responsible for governing the church; but a few have the special task of teaching God's people. These are the ones that we now call pastors.

Paul lists the qualifications of the overseer (1 Tim 3:1-7) and elder (Tit 1:6-9). They must be persons of good reputation and spirituality.

Occasionally Paul mentions deacons as a second office. He addresses one letter "to all the saints in Christ Jesus at Philippi, together with the overseers and deacons" (Phil 1:1). Elsewhere he lists their qualifications (1 Tim 3:8-13).

The word diakonos can mean servant or minister. But here it seems to be a unique office. However the responsibilities of the deacon are not spelled out by Paul.

The elders or overseers are responsible for the well-being of the church. Preaching and teaching are an essential part of church life (1 Tim 5:17).

But holiness is also vital. When gross wickedness was found in the church at Corinth, Paul told the church to "hand this man over to Satan" and "expel the wicked man from among you" (1 Cor 5:5,13).

Hymenaeus and Alexander were two others who rejected instruction and shipwrecked their faith. These two men Paul "handed over to Satan to be taught not to blaspheme" (1 Tim 1:20).

These are two examples of church discipline in Paul's ministry. Church discipline is important to keep the church pure.

The church is the bride of Christ (Eph 5:25-32). The church is the object of Christ's love. Therefore the church must be pure in all of its life.

Study Questions

1. The church is the body of Christ. What does this tell you about the church?
2. The church is God's building and temple. What does this tell you about the church?
3. What is the significance of the Lord's Supper for Paul?
4. What are the tasks of the elder in 1 Timothy 5:17?
5. What are five qualifications of an elder in 1 Timothy 3:1-7?
6. What does Paul mean when he tells the Corinthians to "get rid of the old yeast" (1 Cor 5:7)?

CHAPTER 19

THE HOLY SPIRIT IN PAUL

The church is the body of Christ. But it is the Holy Spirit that builds this body.

The Spirit of Wisdom

Since the Spirit of God is close to God the Father, the Spirit is able to reveal God's secret wisdom. "No one knows the thoughts of God except the Spirit of God." Therefore we received the Spirit "that we may understand what God has freely given us" (1 Cor 2:11-12). One of the tasks of the Spirit is to reveal God to us.

Paul prays that God may give the Ephesians "the Spirit of wisdom and revelation so that [they] may know him better" (Eph 1:17). The Spirit instructs believers in the Christian faith.

The Spirit also reminds believers of their special status as children of God: "The Spirit himself testifies with our spirit that we are God's children" (Rom 8:16).

Baptized and Filled With The Spirit

A person who believes is baptized by the Holy Spirit. Paul writes: "For we were all baptized by one Spirit into one body . . . and we were all given the one Spirit to drink" (1 Cor 12:13).

A person is baptized by the Spirit when the Holy Spirit enters his or her life and radically changes the person. Baptism with the Spirit occurs at conversion. Baptism with the Spirit is the beginning of the Christian life. Water baptism follows the baptism with the Spirit.

Once a person is baptized by the Spirit, he or she should be filled with the Spirit. Paul tells the Ephesian Christians: "Be filled with the Spirit" (Eph 5:18). The present imperative suggests a life-long process. The Christian life of sanctification is the process of being filled with the Spirit. A person who is filled with the Spirit comes under the dominant influence of the Spirit.

Paul teaches two realms of existence: the realm of the Spirit and the realm of the flesh or the sinful nature:

> For those that are after the flesh mind the things of the flesh,
> but they that are after the Spirit mind the things of the Spirit.
>
> —Rom 8:5

A believer is not in the flesh "but in the Spirit if the Spirit of God lives in you" (Rom 8:9). Such a person will put to death the sinful nature: "if by the Spirit you put to death the deeds of the body, you will live" (Rom 8:13).

A Spirit-filled Christian will exhibit the fruit of the Spirit. "The fruit of the Spirit is love, joy, peace, patience, kindness, goodness, faithfulness, gentleness and self-control" (Gal 5:22-23).

There are nine fruits of the Spirit listed here. Every Christian should have each one of these fruits. The life of sanctification will be characterized by these fruits.

Paul prays for the Ephesians that God "may strengthen you with power through his Spirit in your inner being" (Eph 3:16). The Spirit will help the believer live the Christian life.

Spiritual Gifts

Every Christian must have each one of the fruits of the Spirit. But the Spirit will also give a believer one or more of the spiritual gifts.

There are two Greek words for spiritual gift. A *charisma* (pl., *charismata*) is a gift. In Romans, Paul says that "we have different gifts according to the grace given us" (Rom 12:6). To the Corinthians, Paul says, "There are different kinds of gifts, but the same Spirit" (1 Cor 12:4). Peter also speaks of such gifts (1 Pet 4:10).

Sometimes such a gift is called a *pneumatikon* (pl., *pneumatika*) or a spiritual thing (or gift). Paul introduces the section on these gifts with the words: "now about spiritual gifts, I do not want you to be ignorant" (1 Cor 12:1). Later he urges the Corinthians to "desire spiritual gifts" (1 Cor 14:1).

There are five lists of the spiritual gifts in Paul and one in Peter. Romans has a list of seven charismata: prophesying, serving, teaching, encouraging, giving, leading and showing mercy (Rom 12:6-8).

Ephesians has a list of five gifts. Christ "gave some to be apostles, some to be prophets, some to be evangelists, and some to be pastors and teachers" (Eph 4:11).

Peter has a list of two charismata: speaking the words of God and serving (1 Pet 4:10-11).

In the first letter to Corinth, there are three lists of spiritual gifts. The first list has nine gifts: the word of wisdom, the word of knowledge, faith, healing, miracles, prophecy, distinguishing spirits, tongues, and interpreting tongues (1 Cor 12:8-10).

Later, we find apostles, prophets, teachers, workers of miracles, gifts of healing, helping, administering and speaking in tongues (1 Cor 12:28).

Then, we find apostles, prophets, teachers, miracle-workers, healing, tongues and interpretation of tongues (1 Cor 12:29-30).

A few things become evident from these six lists.[1] First, there is a huge diversity of gifts. No two of these lists is the same. As a matter of fact, a comprehensive list of spiritual gifts will go beyond the gifts listed here. How many spiritual gifts are there? John Stott said: "our God is a God of rich and colorful diversity."[2] There is an infinite number of possible gifts.

Second, not all the gifts are miraculous. Some of the gifts are rather ordinary like serving, helping and giving. But they are all vital for the well-being of the church.

Third, there is sometimes a correlation between spiritual gifts and natural talents. Some people have the talent or gift of speaking; others are good administrators; others have a generous and giving heart.

Fourth, there seems to be no special order of priority in the gifts. Speaking in tongues, for example, does not occur in three of the lists; it is toward the bottom of the other three lists.

One cannot claim that the speaking in tongues is more important than the other gifts. It is wrong to say that the person who speaks in tongues is more holy or more Christian than the person who does not speak in tongues. Tongue-speaking is not at the top of any of Paul's lists of the spiritual gifts.

It is important to remember the purpose of the gifts. God gave spiritual gifts to believers to build up the church. Christ gave gifts "to prepare God's people for works of service, so that the body of Christ may be built up" (Eph 4:12). The purpose is "so that the church may be edified" (1 Cor 14:5).

The source of the gifts is the Spirit of God. All the gifts "are the work of one and the same Spirit, and he gives them to each person, just as he determines" (1 Cor 12:11).

---

[1]See J. Stott, *Baptism and Fullness*, pp. 87-90.
[2]J. Stott, *Baptism and Fullness*, p. 89.

Every believer will receive at least one gift. Paul says above that the Spirit gives them "to each person" (1 Cor 12:11). Since the members of the body of Christ are diverse, the gifts that each person will receive will also be diverse (see Rom 12:4-6).

The Holy Spirit is the Spirit of sanctification. The Spirit leads a believer in his or her Christian life. The Spirit is also the one who builds the church through the gifts of the believers.

Study Questions

1. What is the special role of the Holy Spirit in 1 Corinthians 2:9-15?
2. What is the relation between water baptism and Spirit baptism?
3. Contrast the two realms of existence described by Paul in Romans 8:5-9.
4. What is the relation between the fruits of the Spirit and the gifts of the Spirit?
5. What is the purpose of the spiritual gifts?
6. What is your spiritual gift or gifts?

CHAPTER 20

PAULINE ESCHATOLOGY

Paul's entire life and theology were motivated by the expectation of the return of Christ. His entire theology has an eschatological motivation.

The Day of The Lord

Paul eagerly waited for the day of the Lord. He told the Corinthians not to lack any spiritual gift "as you eagerly wait for our Lord Jesus Christ to be revealed." Jesus will keep them strong so that they may be blameless "on the day of our Lord Jesus Christ" (1 Cor 1:7-8).

The day of the Lord or the day of Jesus Christ will be the final day when Jesus will come in glory to judge the world.

The day of the Lord is future. The false prophets were wrong who said that "the day of the Lord has already come" (2 Thess 2:2). Paul agrees with Jesus when he says that "the day of the Lord will come like a thief in the night" (1 Thess 5:2).

The coming day of the Lord is a motivation for Christian living. Paul prays that the Philippians may be "pure and blameless until the day of Christ" (Phil 1:10). Paul hopes that he can boast of the Corinthian Christians "in the day of the Lord Jesus" (2 Cor 1:14).

Three other terms describe this day. The parousia is the coming of Jesus. Paul uses this word frequently in his letters to the

Thessalonians.[1] Twice Paul speaks of the revelation or *apokalupsis* of Jesus (1 Cor 1:7; 2 Thess 1:7). He also speaks of the appearance or *epiphaneia* of Jesus (2 Thess 2:8; 2 Tim 4:1).

The day of the Lord is the time when Jesus will come or appear and be revealed. All three terms describe the final day at the end of time.

The coming of Jesus will be a loud and noisy coming:

> The Lord himself will come down from heaven, with a loud command, with the voice of the archangel and with the trumpet call of God, and the dead in Christ will rise first.
>
> —1 Thess 4:16

Then, those "who are still alive and are left will be caught up with them in the clouds to meet the Lord in the air" (1 Thess 4:17). Christ will gather all of his own for the final judgment.

The lawless one, or the Antichrist, will then be destroyed. He is the one "whom the Lord Jesus will overthrow with the breath of his mouth and destroy at the appearance of his coming" (2 Thess 2:8).

The wicked too will be judged "on the day he comes to be glorified in his holy people" (2 Thess 1:8-10). But at this same coming the believers will be "gathered to him" (2 Thess 2:1).

Paul expects a single day in the future when Jesus will come and be manifested and judge the world. The day of the Lord will be the end of human history.

The Resurrection

The resurrection of the dead will occur at the second coming of Jesus. When the Lord comes from heaven with a trumpet call, "the dead in Christ will rise first" (1 Thess 4:16).

---

[1] 1 Thess 2:19; 3:13; 4:15; 5:23; 2 Thess 2:1,8.

Paul uses similar language in his first letter to the Corinthians: "For the trumpet will sound, the dead will be raised imperishable, and we will be changed" (1 Cor 15:52).

Paul is unable to describe the nature of the resurrection body, but he knows that it will be imperishable, glorious and powerful (1 Cor 15:42-43).

The belief in the resurrection is an affirmation that the body as well as the spirit is important. Paul looks forward to "the redemption of our bodies" (Rom 8:23). Our life in heaven will not be that of disembodied spirits.

The Last Judgment

At the day of the Lord there will be the final judgment. This is "the day of wrath when God's righteous judgment will be revealed" (Rom 2:5).

In a sense, God is the one who will judge the world (Rom 3:6). But God will judge through Jesus Christ. Jesus is the one "who will judge the living and the dead" (2 Tim 4:1). When the Lord comes, "he will bring to light what is hidden in darkness and will expose the motives of our hearts" (1 Cor 4:5).

We will be judged according to our faith. "All will be condemned who have not believed the truth but have delighted in wickedness" (2 Thess 2:12).

Yet, faith without works is dead. "God will give to each person according to what he has done." To those who do good, "he will give eternal life." But to those who do not do good, "there will be wrath and anger" (Rom 2:6-8). "Faith" without works will bring judgment.

In the end, no one will bring any charge against God's elect. "It is God who justifies. Who is he that condemns?" It is Christ Jesus who died and was raised who is interceding for us (Rom 8:33-34).

The Final Kingdom

Jesus is reigning now. "He must reign until he has put all his enemies under his feet." Then "the end will come when he hands over the kingdom to God the Father." Then, God will be all in all (1 Cor 15:25,24,28).

For Paul the kingdom of God is both present and future. The present kingdom is the present reign of Jesus now. But our expectation is the future kingdom of God.

Paul speaks of our "inheritance in the kingdom of Christ and of God" (Eph 5:5). It is the Father who has qualified us "to share in the inheritance of the saints in light." He brought us "into the kingdom of the Son of his love" (Col 1:12-13). These are references to the future kingdom of God.

We will reign with Christ in the future kingdom. Paul says, "If we endure, we will also reign with him" (2 Tim 2:12). Paul looks to the future time when we will share in Christ's glory (Rom 8:17).

But perhaps the heart of the future kingdom is Jesus himself. While he was still on earth, Paul said that he desired to depart "and be with Christ" (Phil 1:23).

The same desire holds on the day of the Lord. When Jesus comes the dead and the living will join him "and so we will be with the Lord forever" (1 Thess 4:17).

This is Paul's eschatological vision. On earth, through the Spirit, we are in Christ. But in the future we will be with the Lord forever. This is the heart of Paul's theology and eschatology.

Study Questions

1. Describe the second coming of Jesus according to First Thessalonians.
2. Describe the lawless one in 2 Thessalonians 2. How will he be defeated?
3. Why is the resurrection of the body important?
4. Will we be judged according to our faith or our works? Explain.
5. When is Jesus reigning according to 1 Corinthians 15:24-28?

PART V

HEBREWS, GENERAL EPISTLES AND REVELATION

The last nine books of the New Testament are diverse. Each has its own theology that is in harmony with the teachings of the Gospels and of Paul.

The Epistle to the Hebrews is an anonymous work. It is assumed that this letter was written to Jewish Christians because of the many references and allusions to the sacrificial system of the Old Testament. The book of Hebrews has profound insights into the person and work of Christ.

The General Epistles are the seven letters between Hebrews and Revelation. They give an insight into the life of Christians in the pagan Roman Empire.

The book of Revelation was written to encourage Christians who were being persecuted in the Roman Empire. The book contains many visions to reassure the suffering Christian. The book of Revelation speaks of the reign of Christ both now and in the future.

CHAPTER 21

THE BLOOD OF JESUS IN HEBREWS

The book of Hebrews is an important New Testament source for understanding who Jesus is and what he accomplished on the cross. This book was written to remind the early church how to respond to Jesus.

The Son of God

The book of Hebrews "has an explicit, high christology."[1] The first chapter of the book stresses the pre-existence and divinity of Christ. At the start we read: "The Son is the radiance of God's glory and the exact representation of his being" (Heb 1:3).

Jesus Christ was active in creation: "In the beginning, O Lord, you laid the foundations of the earth, and the heavens are the work of your hands" (Heb 1:10).

After his saving work, Jesus was exalted to a special position of authority. Then he sat down at the right hand of God (Heb 1:3).

But Jesus too is God. The author says of Jesus, "Your throne, O God, will last for ever and ever" (Heb 1:8). Even the angels will worship Christ (Heb 1:6). Jesus is superior to the angels.

------

[1]G.E. Ladd, *A Theology of the New Testament*, p. 623.

But Jesus is also fully human. Only one who is human can understand us and can die for us. Our high priest "has been tempted in every way, just as we are—yet was without sin" (Heb 4:15).

Just as humans have flesh and blood, so Jesus "shared in their humanity so that by his death he might destroy him who holds the power of death" (Heb 2:14).

The book of Hebrews teaches that Jesus Christ is fully divine and human.

The Priest and His Blood

Two metaphors are used to describe Jesus' work. Jesus is both the great high priest and he is also the sacrifice.

This epistle contrasts the sacrificial system of the Old Testament with that of the new covenant. In the old covenant, the priest was required to make sacrifices frequently; but in the new covenant Jesus the high priest made only one great and lasting sacrifice.

Jesus is called a priest after the order of Melchizedek, who is considered greater than the levitical priests (Heb 7:4-10). "Unlike the other high priests, he does not need to offer sacrifices day after day." But "he sacrificed for [the people's] sins once for all when he offered himself" (Heb 7:27).

Paradoxically, Jesus is both the priest and the sacrifice. In this context Hebrews speaks of the blood of Christ. The blood of Christ is a metaphor for his death. Christ "entered the holy place once for all by his blood" (Heb 9:12). It is "the blood of Christ" that cleanses our consciences (Heb 9:14).

As in Paul, the blood of Christ is not a magical formula. The blood of Christ is his sacrifice that paid for our sins and gives us holiness. This is clear later in the same chapter: "without the shedding of blood there is no forgiveness" (Heb 9:22).

The background for this last statement is the sacrificial system of the Old Testament. Sin and guilt offerings were sacrifices of expiation: the death of the animal removed the guilt of sins. The death of Jesus on the cross was also a sacrifice of expiation.

Three words in Hebrews describe the effect of Jesus' sacrifice. The blood of Jesus purifies, sanctifies and perfects the believer.[2]

First, Jesus made "purification for sins" (Heb 1:3). The blood of Christ purifies or cleanses our consciences (Heb 9:14). And, "the law requires that nearly everything be cleansed with blood, and without the shedding of blood there is no forgiveness" (Heb 9:22).

Purification or cleansing in this context means justification or the forgiveness of sins.[3] We are purified or cleansed when our sins are removed. This is justification by faith.

Second, "we have been sanctified [made holy] through the sacrifice of the body of Jesus Christ once for all" (Heb 10:10). It is the blood of the covenant that sanctifies a believer (Heb 10:29). And, "Jesus suffered outside the city to sanctify the people through his own blood" (Heb 13:12).

Here sanctification means to consecrate or make holy ceremonially. In this sense, sanctification is the taking away of our sins resulting in a ceremonial holiness. This is similar to the legal justification of which Paul talks.

The third concept is unique to Hebrews. A believer is made perfect through the death of Christ. The sacrifices of the old covenant cannot make perfect the consciences of the worshiper (Heb 9:9). It is only the sacrifice of Jesus that makes us perfect: "by one sacrifice he has made perfect forever those who are being made holy" (Heb 10:14).

---

[2]G.E. Ladd, *A Theology of the New Testament*, pp. 627-28.

[3]G.E. Ladd says, "Forgiveness of sins is a synonym for this purification" (*A Theology of the New Testament*, p. 628).

This last reference highlights the "already"-"not yet" tension of a believer. Through the cross the believer is made holy or perfect. This is justification by faith. But our entire life is a process of being made holy. This is what is traditionally called the sanctification of the believer.

The death of Christ, then, purifies, sanctifies and perfects the believer.

The Response of Faith

The book of Hebrews contains the great chapter on faith (Hebrews 11). The book was written to encourage the reader to respond in faith.

If Jesus is so much greater than Moses and the angels, should we not listen to him? We should be warned by the example of the Israelites in the desert not to harden our hearts (Heb 3:7-19).

Instead, we should have faith.

> Now faith is being sure of what we hope for and certain of what
> we do not see. This is what the ancients were commended for.
> —Heb 11:1-2

The eleventh chapter of Hebrews gives some great examples of those who believed in the Old Testament.

> Since we are surrounded by such a great cloud of witnesses . . .
> let us fix our eyes on Jesus, the author and perfecter of our faith.
> —Heb 12:1-2

This faith must be accompanied by love. The book concludes with the instruction: "Keep on loving each other as brothers" (Heb 13:1).

The death of Christ purifies or justifies a believer. But a Christian must live a life of holiness and love. There must be a correspondence between our status as purified or holy persons and our Christian life.

Study Questions

1. What does the first chapter of Hebrews tell us about Jesus?
2. Why is it important that Jesus was fully human?
3. In Hebrews 9:14, what is the blood of Christ that cleanses our consciences?
4. How does the death of Christ purify, sanctify and perfect the believer?
5. How is sanctification both an act of Christ and a requirement for the believer?

CHAPTER 22

CHRISTIANS IN A HOSTILE WORLD

Christianity began in the pagan world of the Roman Empire. Often this environment was hostile to Christians.

Seven letters at the end of the New Testament were written to Christians in this hostile pagan environment. These letters are commonly called the General or Catholic Epistles. ("Catholic" means "universal.") These letters are general in the sense that most of them have a general audience.

These letters are James, 1 & 2 Peter, 1, 2 & 3 John and Jude. They were all written in the first century.

A Pagan And Hostile World

Christianity arose in the pagan Roman Empire. There was widespread idolatry in this empire. There was emperor worship. There was gross immorality.

Christians were "aliens and strangers" in this pagan world (1 Pet 2:11). Therefore, John writes, "do not be surprised if the world hates you" (1 Jn 3:13).

Peter spoke of the lifestyle of the pagans (*ta ethnē*) who were living "in debauchery, lust, drunkenness, orgies, carousing and detestable idolatry" (1 Pet 4:3). The Christians, in contrast, were to live "good lives among the pagans" (1 Pet 2:12).

Often in the first century it was illegal to be a Christian. Consequently the Christians were sometimes persecuted for their faith. Often Christians were persecuted because they did not partake in the sinful practices of the pagans.

Peter writes, "Do not be surprised at the painful trial you are suffering . . . . However, if you suffer as a Christian, do not be ashamed" (1 Pet 4:12,16).

James writes of "trials of many kinds." But "blessed is the one who perseveres under trial" (Jas 1:2,12). James speaks of Job who is "an example of patience in the face of suffering" (Jas 5:10-11).

In the early church in the Roman Empire, there was also a constant problem of false teachers. Gnosticism and Docetism, for example, were theologies that denied the humanity of Jesus since they believed that the flesh was evil.

John calls these false teachers "antichrists." An antichrist "denies that Jesus is the Messiah" (1 Jn 2:22).

> Every spirit that acknowledges that Jesus Christ has come in the flesh is from God, but every spirit that does not acknowledge Jesus is not from God. This is the spirit of the antichrist.
>
> —1 Jn 4:2-3

Peter and Jude speak of false prophets who lead many astray. These are teachers who teach false doctrines and who preach immorality (2 Pet 2:1-3; Jude 1:4).

The General Letters or Epistles were written in this context to encourage the believers of the early church.

You are Holy

The General Epistles presuppose that a believer in Jesus Christ is holy or set apart by one's faith in Jesus. The basis of our holiness is Christ's death on the cross.

Believers in Jesus "were redeemed . . . with the precious blood of Christ, a lamb without blemish or defect" (1 Pet 1:18-19). Consequently, a believer is holy.

The Christian church is holy like Israel in the Old Testament. Peter writes: "But you are a chosen people, a royal priesthood, a holy nation, a people belonging to God" (1 Pet 2:9). Like Israel in the Old Testament, Christians are "God's elect" (1 Pet 1:1).

Christians are also children of God. John writes,

> How great is the love the Father has lavished on us that we should be called children of God! And that is what we are!
>
> —1 Jn 3:1

Through faith a believer is a child of God. "Everyone who believes that Jesus is the Messiah is born of God" (1 Jn 5:1).

John also tells us that a believer has "an anointing from the Holy One" (1 Jn 2:20). If we believe in Jesus, we are holy. This is an indicative statement of fact. It is parallel to Paul's teaching on justification. A believer is just and holy before God.

Therefore, be Holy!

Peter says that the church is holy: "you are . . . a holy nation" (1 Pet 2:9). But at the same time, Peter tells the believers to be holy: "be holy in all you do." As God said in Leviticus, "Be holy, because I am holy" (1 Pet 1:15). So are the Christians holy, or are they not holy?

Because of the atoning sacrifice of Jesus, believers are cleansed from their sins and holy. But a Christian must practice sanctification or holiness in his or her life. We are to be holy as God is holy.

Love (*agapē*) is the primary ethical quality of a believer. Peter writes: "love one another deeply, from the heart" (1 Pet 1:22). Again, "love each other deeply, because love covers over a multitude of sins" (1 Pet 4:8).

Agapē love is one of the main themes of First John. John tells us that "God is love" (1 Jn 4:16). The great example of love is Jesus Christ:

> This is how we know what love is: Jesus Christ laid down his life for us. And we ought to lay down our lives for our brothers.
>
> —1 Jn 3:16

But holiness also means keeping God's commands. John writes, "This is love for God: to obey his commands" (1 Jn 5:3). John says,

> We know that we have come to know him if we obey his commands. . . . Whoever claims to live in him must walk as Jesus did.
>
> —1 Jn 2:3,6

James, using slightly different language, talks of doing good works (*erga*). Too many Christians claim to have faith but do not have the deeds or works to prove it. James writes, "What good is it . . . if a person claims to have faith but has no deeds? Can such faith save him?" (Jas 2:14).

Abraham, for example, is known for his faith that justified him. But Abraham's faith was not dead. Instead, his faith produced good works. James then asks,

> Was not Abraham our father justified by works when he offered his son Isaac upon the altar? You see that faith was active along with his works, and faith was completed by works.
>
> —Jas 2:21-22

Is James contradicting Paul? We think not. Instead, both Paul and James teach that our faith must produce good works. Both Paul and

James agree that we are *justified by faith that produces works.* We are justified by a living faith, not a dead one.

If we are in Christ, we are justified and sanctified. If we are a holy people, we must live holy lives.

In the end, the key to holy living is a personal relationship with God. John writes,

> If anyone acknowledges that Jesus is the Son of God, God lives in him and he in God. . . . God is love. Whoever lives in love lives in God, and God in him.
>
> —1 Jn 4:15-16

Faith in Jesus unites us with Christ and gives us the holiness of justification and the holiness of sanctification.

The Day of the Lord

The General Epistles were written in a hostile environment. The writers of these epistles looked forward to the return of Jesus.

James urges the believers to "be patient . . . until the Lord's coming" (Jas 5:7). Peter reminds his readers that "when the Chief Shepherd appears, you will receive the crown of glory that will never fade away" (1 Pet 5:4).

The second coming of Jesus is an incentive for ethical living. James writes, "As believers in our glorious Lord Jesus Christ, don't show favoritism" (Jas 2:1). Peter writes, "Prepare your minds for action; be self-controlled; set your hope fully on the grace to be given you when Jesus Christ is revealed" (1 Pet 1:13). John writes, "Continue in him so that when he appears we may be confident and unashamed before him at his coming" (1 Jn 2:28).

In his second epistle, Peter says that "the day of the Lord will come like a thief." Therefore, "you ought to live holy and godly lives as you look forward to the day of God and speed its coming" (2 Pet 3:10-12).

That is future eschatology. But already we have overcome the world. John says, "Everyone born of God has overcome the world. This is the victory that has overcome the world, even our faith" (1 Jn 5:4).

There will be suffering in this world. But God has already given us the victory. We also believe that Jesus is coming again to reward those who believe in him and are holy.

Study Questions

1. Describe the social and political situation of the General Epistles.
2. How are Christians already holy?
3. Explain the fact that Christians are both holy and not holy.
4. Is justification by faith or by faith and works, according to James? Explain.
5. What does 2 Peter 2 say about the day of the Lord?

CHAPTER 23

THE REIGN OF THE LAMB

The New Testament concludes with many of the basic themes that we have seen starting with the Synoptic Gospels. The Apocalypse,[1] or book of Revelation, emphasizes the death of Christ, the downfall of Satan and the reign of Jesus. But its language is highly symbolic and metaphorical. It is wrong to take the picture language too literally.

The Apocalypse was written to comfort the early church that was being persecuted by the Roman Empire. Where are the martyrs who were killed for their faith? Who is in control of world history? Revelation proclaims the reign of Christ despite the power of the evil Roman Empire.

The Blood of the Lamb

The christology of Revelation is presented in picture language. Who is Jesus? He is "like a son of man" with a gold sash around his robe, with white hair, blazing eyes and bronze-like feet, holding seven stars, with a sharp sword coming from his mouth (Rev 1:12-16).

This is a symbolic picture of Jesus as the glorious son of man. Jesus is the glorious messianic figure predicted in Daniel 7. Jesus is the royal messiah.

---

[1]The first word of the book of Revelation is *apokalupsis*, which means "revelation."

A similar description of Jesus' majesty is found earlier in this first chapter of Revelation. Jesus is "the faithful witness, the firstborn from the dead, and the ruler of the kings of the earth" (Rev. 1:5). Jesus' pre-eminence is clearly stated here.

In another vision, the presence of Jesus is announced: "See, the lion of the tribe of Judah, the root of David, has triumphed" (Rev 5:5). The lion of Judah is the messianic king from the line of David.

So John turns to see the lion. But he sees "a lamb, looking as if it had been slain" (Rev 5:6). This is the mystery of the Gospel, starting from the Synoptics and reaching to Revelation. Jesus is both a lion and a lamb; Jesus is both the king and the suffering servant.

Jesus is called a lamb (*arnion*) 29 times in Revelation. Here a theme of John from his Gospel is picked up. At the beginning of that Gospel, Jesus is called "the Lamb of God, who takes away the sin of the world" (Jn 1:29). At the end of that Gospel, Jesus is crucified as the Passover lamb (Jn 19).

The imagery of a sacrificial lamb is derived from the Old Testament. The blood of the Passover lamb at the Exodus averted evil. The blood of lambs and other animals atoned for sin.

Revelation also speaks of the blood of Jesus. What is the function of the blood of Jesus? Should we cover our cars with the blood of Jesus?

At the beginning of the book, we learn that Jesus "freed us from our sins by his blood" (Rev 1:5). Later we discover that Jesus with his blood purchased for God people of every tribe and nation (Rev 5:9). Again we see that the persecuted Christians "washed their robes and made them white in the blood of the lamb" (Rev 7:14). Finally we note that the believers triumphed over Satan "by the blood of the lamb" (Rev 12:11).

Clearly the blood of Jesus has power. But what kind of power? According to the texts above, the blood of Jesus cleanses us from our sins. The blood of Jesus redeems the believers.

In short, the blood of Jesus is powerful because it is atoning and it takes away our sins. The blood of Jesus is not a magical formula; rather, the blood of Jesus refers to the expiatory sacrifice of Jesus that removes our sins. And this is bad news for Satan.

The Downfall of Satan

The Apocalypse proclaims the ultimate triumph of believers and the defeat of Satan. So when was Satan defeated?

In the Synoptic Gospels, we saw that the downfall of Satan began at the first coming of Jesus. When the 72 disciples came back with the incredible news that even the demons submit to them in Jesus' name, Jesus said, "I saw Satan fall like lightning from heaven" (Lk 10:18). During Jesus' earthly ministry, he waged serious warfare against Satan, casting out the demons.

We also saw that when Jesus was lifted up, "the prince of this world [was] driven out" (Jn 12:31). We also observed that Jesus "disarmed the powers and authorities . . . triumphing over them by the cross" (Col 2:14-15).

Already at the cross Satan was defeated; but his final defeat is still in the future. In the book of Revelation we again have this "already"-"not yet" tension.

Revelation 12 is a key passage. There the dragon—or Satan— attacks the woman who gives birth to a male child. The child—or Jesus —is taken up to heaven. Then there is war between the angels and Satan, and Satan is hurled to the earth. After this Satan wages war on the woman, who is the church.

When was Satan hurled to the earth? The sequence of events and the hymn of praise suggest that Satan was hurled to the earth when Jesus paid for all of our sins. The believers triumphed over Satan "by the blood of the lamb" (Rev 12:11).

The testimony of Revelation is the same as that of Paul. In the first letter to Corinth, Paul asks,

> Where, O death is your victory? Where, O death, is your sting? The sting of death is sin, and the power of sin is the law. But thanks be to God who gives us the victory through our Lord Jesus Christ.
>
> —1 Cor 15:55-57

Satan and death were defeated when the demands of the law were satisfied on the cross.

This may throw light on the difficult chapter of Revelation 20. Before the reign of Christ, Satan was seized and chained and thrown into the Abyss. Is this a symbolic picture of the defeat of Satan at the cross? Did the binding of Satan occur at the cross?

The rest of the New Testament suggests that the great defeat of Satan occurred at the cross and resurrection. Satan was bound with a chain. But the chain, admittedly, is a long chain.

The Reign of Christ

The good news for the persecuted Christians in the Roman Empire—and today—is that Jesus is reigning now. The Lamb has triumphed by his blood and he is now the lion who rules.

The Lamb who was slain has the power to open the seals: "Worthy is the Lamb, who was slain, to receive power and wealth and wisdom and strength and honor and glory and praise" (Rev 5:12).

After Satan was hurled to the earth, a loud voice said, "Now have come the salvation and the power and the kingdom of our God, and the authority of his Messiah" (Rev 12:10).

Jesus Christ is not just the faithful witness and the firstborn from the dead but also "the ruler of the kings of the earth" (Rev 1:5). Jesus is king—now! Jesus reigns over the evil powers of this earth—now!

This was the message of Jesus when he first came to the earth: "The kingdom of God is near" (Mk 1:15). The Synoptic Gospels taught the presence of the kingdom of God at the first coming of Jesus.

After his resurrection and ascension, Jesus is now seated at the right hand of God the Father, reigning over the earth. Jesus received power when God "raised Christ from the dead and seated him at the right hand in the heavenly realms" (Eph 1:20). Jesus is reigning now!

This testimony of the New Testament may help us to understand Revelation 20. There we read that Jesus is reigning with the martyrs for a thousand years.

The number thousand is probably symbolic. A thousand years is a very long period of time. The place of the reign is not stated but presumed. We presume that Jesus is reigning in heaven, as the rest of the New Testament suggests.

So when is the thousand-year reign of Jesus? It is possible that the thousand-year reign is the reign of Christ between his first and second coming.

After Satan was defeated at the cross, the reign of Christ began. It will continue until the end of time, when Jesus "hands over the kingdom to God the Father, after he has destroyed all dominion, authority and power" (1 Cor 15:24).

The last two chapters of Revelation describe the future eschatological kingdom. Words cannot describe that kingdom.

Pictures only give impressions of the glory of the future kingdom. The present kingdom of Christ is a foretaste of this future kingdom.

The New Testament began with the kingdom of God: "Repent, for the kingdom of heaven is near" (Mt 3:2). The New Testament now closes with the same kingdom. This present and future kingdom of God is a central theme of the New Testament.

Study Questions

1.   What does the first chapter of Revelation teach us about Jesus?
2.   How is Jesus like a lamb?
3.   Describe the power of the blood of the lamb.
4.   When was Satan defeated? Explain.
5.   When and where is the thousand-year reign of Jesus?
6.   How is the book of Revelation a comfort for the persecuted Christian today?

BIBLIOGRAPHY

Bultmann, Rudolf. *Kerygma and Myth*. New York: Harper and Row, 1961. Translated by R. Fuller.

Bultmann, Rudolf. *Theology of the New Testament*. New York: Scribner, 1955. Translated by K. Grobel.

Cullmann, Oscar. *Christ and Time*. Philadelphia: Westminster, 1964. Translated by F. Filson.

Dodd, C.H. *The Parables of the Kingdom*. Revised edition. Glasgow: Collins, 1978.

Green, Michael. *I Believe in the Holy Spirit*. Revised edition. London: Hodder and Stoughton, 1985.

Guthrie, Donald. *New Testament Theology*. Downers Grove: Inter-Varsity Press, 1981.

Imasogie, Osadolor. *Guidelines for Christian Theology in Africa*. Achimota: African Christian Press, 1983.

Jeremias, Joachim. *New Testament Theology: The Proclamation of Jesus*. New York: Charles Scribner, 1971. Translated by J. Bowden.

Kümmel, W.G. *The Theology of the New Testament according to Its Major Witnesses*. Nashville: Abingdon, 1973. Translated by J. Steely.

Ladd, George E. *A Theology of the New Testament*. Revised edition. Grand Rapids: Eerdmans, 1993.

Marshall, I.H. *New Testament Theology*. Downers Grove: Inter-Varsity Press, 2004.

Morris, Leon. *New Testament Theology*. Grand Rapids: Zondervan, 1986.

Morris, Leon. *The Apostolic Preaching of the Cross*. Grand Rapids: Eerdmans, 1956.

Murray, John. *Redemption—Accomplished and Applied*. Grand Rapids: Eerdmans, 1955.

Neill, S. *Jesus through Many Eyes: Introduction to the Theology of the New Testament*. Nashville: Abingdon, 1976.

Palmer, Timothy. *A Theology of the Old Testament*. Bukuru: Africa Christian Textbooks, 2011.

Ratzinger, Joseph. *Jesus of Nazareth*. 2007.

Ridderbos, Herman. *Paul: An Outline of His Theology*. Grand Rapids: Eerdmans, 1975. Translated by J. De Witt.

Schreiner, Thomas. *New Testament Theology: Magnifying God in Christ*. Grand Rapids: Baker, 2008.

Smedes, Lewis. *All Things Made New*. Grand Rapids: Eerdmans, 1970.

Stott, John. *Baptism and Fullness*. Downers Grove: Inter-Varsity Press, 1976.

Vos, Geerhardus. *The Pauline Eschatology*. Grand Rapids: Eerdmans, 1952.

Westerholm, Stephen. *Perspectives Old and New on Paul*. Grand Rapids: Eerdmans, 2004.

www.ingramcontent.com/pod-product-compliance
Lightning Source LLC
Chambersburg PA
CBHW071150130726
47998CB00002B/462